Second Edition

SPANISH VERB DRILLS

by

Vivienne Bey
Ball State University

in collaboration with
Beatrice Concheff
University of Wisconsin

PASSPORT BOOKS
a division of *NTC Publishing Group*
Lincolnwood, Illinois USA

1993 Printing

Contents

Introduction

Spanish Verb Drills is designed to help learners develop mastery of the Spanish verb system. Created to supplement the oral and written verb practice offered by standard Spanish-language textbooks, it provides students at all levels with the drill and review needed to grasp the tenses and conjugations of Spanish verbs.

Models at the beginning of each unit establish the patterns to be reinforced in the *Para practicar* drills, the *Aplicación* exercises, and the Mastery Tests. In addition, the four-part *Repaso general* allows students to test themselves for overall control of the Spanish verb system.

Combining the features of a workbook, textbook, and self-study manual, *Spanish Verb Drills* clearly and systematically explains the workings of the Spanish verb system, while providing numerous and varied exercises for thorough practice of each point covered. In addition, the Answer Key at the back of this edition provides valuable support when learners need to clarify a concept immediately.

Covering verb tenses ranging from the present indicative to the imperfect subjunctive and offering detailed treatment of stem-changing verbs, orthographic-changing verbs, and irregular verbs, *Spanish Verb Drills* will serve as an important study aid to all those wishing to perfect their knowledge of Spanish verbs. Equally suitable in a Spanish-language course or for self-study, this book effectively clarifies the complexities of this crucial area of Spanish-language study.

Regular Verbs
Present

Spanish verbs are classified into three classes, or *conjugations*, according to the final letters of their infinitives. The present tense of regular verbs is formed by adding the personal endings to the *stem*, which is determined by dropping the *-ar*, *-er*, or *-ir* of the infinitive.

		1	2	3
		*habl*ar to speak	*com*er to eat	*part*ir to leave
yo	habl *o*	I speak, am speaking, do speak	com *o* I eat, etc.	part *o* I leave, etc.
tú	habl *as*	you speak, etc.	com *es* you eat, etc.	part *es* you leave, etc.
Ud.	habl *a*	you speak, etc.	com *e* you eat, etc.	part *e* you leave, etc.
él(ella)	habl *a*	he(she) speaks, etc.	com *e* he(she) eats, etc.	part *e* he(she) leaves, etc.
nosotros	habl *amos*	we speak, etc.	com *emos* we eat, etc.	part *imos* we leave, etc.
vosotros	habl *áis*	you speak, etc.	com *éis* you eat, etc.	part *ís* you leave, etc.
Uds.	habl *an*	you speak, etc.	com *en* you eat, etc.	part *en* you leave, etc.
ellos (ellas)	habl *an*	they speak, etc.	com *en* they eat, etc.	part *en* they leave, etc.

1. Spanish has no equivalent for the English *am* (is, are) or *do* (does) in the present tense. The single verb *hablo* means *I am speaking*, *I do speak*, or *I speak*.

2. The pronoun subject of the Spanish verb is expressed by the ending of the verb. The verb must show this personal ending, even if a subject pronoun or noun is already present in the sentence. The subject pronouns (*yo*, etc.) are seldom used in actual practice, except for *Ud.* and *Uds*. Remember that there are two singular and two plural forms of the second person (you), for informal and formal use. The *tú* and *vosotros* forms of the verb may not be used with the subjects *Ud.* and *Uds.*, or vice versa.

Negative: All Spanish verbs form the negative by placing *no* before the verb.

He eats *come*;   he does not eat *no come*.

Interrogative: All Spanish verbs in the interrogative are identical to the affirmative.

He eats *come*;   does he eat? ¿*come*?

Spanish verbs in the negative-interrogative are identical to the negative.

He does not eat *no come*;   doesn't he eat? ¿*no come*?

Para practicar

All regular verbs with infinitives ending in -ar form the present like *hablar*. Write the present tense of (1) *acabar* to finish, and (2) *tomar* to take.

(1) **acabar**
yo _acabo_ finish
tú _acabas_
Ud. _acaba_
él _acaba_
nosotros _acabamos_
vosotros _____
Uds. _acaban_
ellos _acaban_

(2) **tomar**
yo _tomo_
tú _tomas_
Ud. _toma_
ella _toma_
nosotros _tomamos_
vosotros _____
Uds. _toman_
ellos _toman_

All regular verbs with infinitives in -er form the present like *comer*. Write the present tense of (1) *vender* to sell, and (2) *beber* to drink.

(1) **vender**
yo _vendo_
tú _vendes_
Ud. _vende_
él _vende_
nosotros _vendemos_
vosotros _____
Uds. _venden_
ellos _venden_

(2) **beber**
yo _bebo_
tú _bebes_
Ud. _bebe_
él _bebe_
nosotros _bebemos_
vosotros _____
Uds. _beben_
ellos _beben_

All regular verbs with infinitives in *-ir* form the present like *partir*. Write the present tense of
(1) *vivir* to live, and (2) *recibir* to receive.

(1) **vivir** yo *vivo*   (2) **recibir** yo *recibo*

tú *vives*   tú *recibes*

Ud. *vive*   Ud. *recibe*

él *vive*   él *recibe*

nosotros *vivimos*   nosotros *recibimos*

vosotros   vosotros

Uds. *viven*   Uds. *reciben*

ellos *viven*   ellos *reciben*

Change the infinitives below into the correct form of the present, according to the subject indicated:

yo

estudiar	comprender	temer *(fear)*	necesitar	partir	enseñar
estudio	*comprendo*	*temo*	*necesito*	*parto*	*enseño*

vender
vendo

tú

hablar	asistir	abrir	beber	preguntar	tomar
hablas	*asistes*	*abres*	*bebes*	*preguntas*	*tomas*

escuchar
escuchas

4

Ud.

contestar	abrir	aprender	entrar	leer	vivir
contesta	abre	aprende	entra	lee	vive

comer

come

Juan (what person?)

escribir	estudiar	acabar	temer	partir	comprender
escribe	estudia	acaba	teme	parte	comprende

vender

vende

nosotros

aprender	asistir	tomar	escuchar	hablar	vivir
apendemos	asistimos	tomamos	escuchamos	hablamos	vivimos

temer

tememos

~~vosotros~~ ellas

hablar	asistir	beber	leer	tomar	llevar
hablan	asisten	beben	leen	toman	llevan

enseñar (show)

enseñan

Uds.

comer	escribir	necesitar	entrar	acabar	leer
comen	escriben	necesitan	entran	acaban	leen

vivir

viven

María y Juan (what person?)

temer	llevar	estudiar	preguntar	contestar	comprender
temen	*llevan*	*estudian*	*preguntan*	*contestan*	*comprenden*

partir

parten

Aplicación

A. Write the verb forms in the person indicated by the pronoun:

1. nosotros (tomar) *tomamos*

2. él (aprender) *aprende*

3. ellos (vender) *venden*

4. yo (asistir) *asisto*

5. tú (contestar) *contestas*

6. Ud. (beber) *bebe*

7. nosotras (abrir) *abrimos*

8. ella (necesitar) *necesita*

9. vosotros (tomar) *tomáis*

10. ella (leer) *lee*

11. yo (aprender) *aprendo*

12. nosotros (temer) *tememos*

13. vosotros (recibir) *recibís*

14. ellos (escribir) *escriben*

15. ella (abrir) *abre*

16. nosotros (enseñar) *enseñamos*

17. yo (contestar) *contesto*

18. nosotros (estudiar) *estudiamos*

19. yo (abrir) *abro*

20. ella (tomar) *toma*

21. Ud. (preguntar) *pregunta*

22. ellas (leer) *leen*

23. ellos (recibir) *reciben*

24. tú (temer) *temes*

25. nosotras (leer) *leemos*

B. Change each verb form to the corresponding person of the plural, and translate the plural verb into English:

1. escribo *escribimos*
   we write

2. él contesta *ellos contestan*
   they answer

3. vivo *vivimos*
   we live

4. Ud. necesita *necesitan*
   you need

5. él bebe _beben_
drink

6. aprendes _aprendeís_
learn

7. él vende _venden_
sell

8. asisto _asistimos_
help attend

9. Ud. enseña _enseñan_
teach

10. abres _abrís_
open

11. Ud. comprende _comprenden_
understand

12. ella escucha _eschuchan_
listen

13. temes _teméis_
fear

14. ella pregunta _preguntan_
ask

15. Ud. lee _leen_
read

16. tomo _tomamos_
take

17. recibo _recibimos_
receive

18. él estudia _estudian_
study

19. necesito _necesitamos_
need

20. escribes _escribís_
write

Mastery Test

estudiar to study	*trabajar* to work	esconder to hide
necesitar to need	*comprender* to understand	*vivir* to live
contestar to answer	*beber* to drink	*recibir* to receive
preguntar to ask	*vender* to sell	*asistir* to attend
enseñar to teach	*aprender* to learn	*abrir* to open
escuchar to listen	*temer* to fear	*escribir* to write
tomar to take	*leer* to read	*unir* to join, unite
entrar to enter	*creer* to believe	

Translate the following, using the above list of infinitives:

1. we answer _contestamos_

2. you sell _vende_

3. he is asking _él pregunta_

4. they do sell _venden_

5. we do not need _no necesitamos_

6. we study _estudiamos_

7. I am learning _aprendo_

8. do they listen? _¿escuchen ellos?_

9. he is not reading _él no lee_

10. you are not entering _no entra_

11. we work _trabajamos_

12. do you write? _¿escribe?_

13. they do ask _preguntan_

14. you are taking _Uds toman_

15. I sell _vendo_

16. she does not work _ella no trabaja_

17. they do not believe _no creen_

18. they hide _esconden_

19. he writes _él escribe_

20. do you fear? _¿teme? ¿temes?_

21. we are living _vivimos_

22. he teaches _él enseña_

23. she fears _ella teme_

24. you receive _recibe_

25. he is opening _él abre_

26. they do not take _no toman_

27. we attend _asistamos_

28. is he selling? _¿vende él?_

29. I study _estudio_

30. I believe _creo_

31. they unite _unen_

32. they are not opening _no abren_

33. you teach _tú enseñas_

34. he attends _él asiste_

35. we ask _preguntamos_

36. do you learn? _¿apprenda?_

37. she drinks _ella bebe_

38. are you studying? _¿estudias?_

39. you live _vive_

40. they enter _entran_

Imperfect

The imperfect is formed by adding the appropriate endings to the stem.

	1		*2*		*3*
	hablar		**comer**		**partir**
yo	habl *aba* I was speaking,	com *ía* I was eating,	part *ía* I was leaving,
tú	habl *abas* used to speak	com *ías* used to eat	part *ías* used to leave
Ud.	habl *aba*	com *ía*	part *ía*
él(ella)	habl *aba*	com *ía*	part *ía*
nosotros	habl *ábamos*	com *íamos*	part *íamos*
vosotros	habl *abais*	com *íais*	part *íais*
Uds.	habl *aban*	com *ían*	part *ían*
ellos	habl *aban*	com *ían*	part *ían*

Note: The imperfect is translated as *I spoke* or *I did speak* in actual practice as well as the meanings given above. For drill purposes, however, this manual will consider *I was speaking* or *I used to speak* (*you*, *he*, etc.) as translations of the imperfect. Interrogative imperfect is *was I speaking* or *did I speak* and negative imperfect is *I was not speaking* or *I did not speak*.

All forms of the imperfect of *-er* and *-ir* verbs must have a written accent. Because first- and third-person singular forms are identical, context determines the subject for them.

Para practicar

Write the form of the imperfect that corresponds to the subject indicated:

yo

tomar	meter	vivir	comprar	sentir	viajar
tomaba	*metía*	*vivía*	*compraba*	*sentía*	*viajaba*

correr

corría

tú

aprender	subir	pasar	guardar	coser	esperar
aprendías	*subías*	*pasabas*	*guardabas*	*cosías*	*esperabas*

acabar

acababas

Ud.

tocar	amar	saber	jugar	viajar	comprender
tocaba	_amaba_	_sabía_	_jugaba_	_viajaba_	_comprendía_

escribir
escribía

María

echar	preparar	leer	vivir	abrir	correr
echaba	_preparaba_	_leía_	_vivía_	_abría_	_corría_

trabajar
trabajaba

nosotros

estudiar	vender	subir	comprender	abrir	preparar
estudiábamos	_vendíamos_	_subíamos_	_comprendíamos_	_abríamos_	_preparábamos_

tomar
tomábamos

vosotros

escribir	trabajar	comer	beber	recibir	comprar
_____	_____	_____	_____	_____	_____

llevar
_____

Juan y Ud. (What person?)

pasar	caminar	responder	subir	hablar	abrir
pasaban	_caminaban_	_respondían_	_subían_	_hablaban_	_abrían_

sacar
sacaban

ellos

acabar	salir	contestar	vivir	guardar	correr
acababan	*salían*	*contestaban*	*vivían*	*guardaban*	*corrían*

viajar

viajaban

Aplicación

A. Write the imperfect form in the person indicated by the subject:

1. él (hablar) *hablaba*
2. Elena y yo (vivir) *vivíamos*
3. ella (saber) *sabía*
4. Uds. (conocer) *conocían*
5. los niños (pedir) *pedían*
6. nosotros (correr) *corríamos*
7. tú (partir) *partías*
8. yo (pasar) *pasaba*
9. vosotros (esperar) _____
10. Uds. (acabar) *acababan*
11. Ud. (caminar) *caminaba*
12. él (comprender) *comprendía*
13. Juan y Pedro (tomar) *tomaban*
14. yo (escribir) *escribía*
15. Ud. (amar) *amaba*
16. vosotros (conocer) _____

B. Change to imperfect and translate new form into English:

1. contestamos *contestábamos. we answered*
2. vendes *vendías, you were selling*
3. él pregunta *preguntaba, he was asking*
4. aprendo *aprendía I was learning*
5. ellos escuchan *escuchaban used to listen*
6. Ud. escribe *escribía*
7. ellos aprenden *aprendían*
8. Ud. estudia *estudí*
9. vivimos _____
10. él teme _____
11. él abre _____
12. ellos enseñan _____
13. él asiste _____
14. tomamos _____
15. leo _____
16. Uds. beben _____

17. tú (beber) _bebías_

18. nosotros (comprar) _comprábamos_

19. ellos (subir) _subían_

20. yo (correr) _corría_

21. ella (responder) _respondía_

22. tú (guardar) _guardabas_

23. Ud. (aprender) _aprendía_

24. Juan y él (llevar) _llevaban_

25. vosotros (pasar) _____

17. temo _____

18. ellos reciben _____

19. necesito _____

20. Uds. viven _____

21. abrimos _____

22. contestáis _____

23. tomas _____

24. él bebe _____

25. abrís _____

Mastery Test

Write the Spanish that corresponds to the English verb forms, selecting the correct verb from the list on page 6.

1. they used to live _____

2. we were working _____

3. you (s., fam.) were not selling _____

_____

4. we used to live _____

5. they did not need _____

6. you (s., for.) were learning _____

_____

7. he used to believe _____

8. you (pl., fam.) were asking _____

_____

9. I used to fear _____

10. did you (s., fam.) understand? _____

_____

11. she was teaching _____

12. you (pl., for.) used to take _____

_____

13. we were not listening _____

_____

14. he used to sell _____

15. you (pl., for.) were opening _____

_____

16. were they receiving? _____

17. we were attending _____

18. you (s., fam.) used to study _____

_____

19. he was reading _____

20. they were living _____

21. you (pl., for.) were not hiding _____

_____

22. I used to receive _____

23. they did not understand _____

_____

24. I was eating _____

25. you (s., for.) used to sell _____

_____

26. you (s., fam.) were not taking _____

_____

27. they were listening _____

28. was he attending? _____

29. you (pl., fam.) used to need _____

_____

30. she was answering _____

_____

Preterit

The preterit is formed in regular verbs by adding the preterit endings to the stem.

	1 **hablar**		*2* **comer**		*3* **partir**
yo	habl *é* I spoke, I did speak	com *í* I ate,		part *í* I left, did
tú	habl *aste* you spoke, etc.	com *iste* did eat		part *iste* leave
Ud.	habl *ó*	com *ió*		part *ió*
él(ella)	habl *ó*	com *ió*		part *ió*
nosotros	habl *amos*	com *imos*		part *imos*
vosotros	habl *asteis*	com *isteis*		part *isteis*
Uds.	habl *aron*	com *ieron*		part *ieron*
ellos	habl *aron*	com *ieron*		part *ieron*

Note: First- and third-person singular forms in all conjugations require a written accent. First-person plural forms of *-ar* and *-ir* verbs are identical to the present. As with the imperfect, endings for *-er* and *-ir* verbs are identical.

In this manual *I spoke* will be translated with the preterit as will *I did speak*. In negative or interrogative verbs, *I did not....* or *did I....* may indicate either imperfect or preterit.

Para practicar

Write the preterit of each verb that corresponds to the subject indicated:

yo

viajar	trabajar	estudiar	comer	vender	insistir
_____	_____	_____	_____	_____	_____

recibir

_____

tú

unir	acabar	comprar	romper	correr	abrir
_____	_____	_____	_____	_____	_____

tomar

_____

Ud.

comer	asistir	echar	preparar	subir	pasar
_____	_____	_____	_____	_____	_____

trabajar

_____

Pepe

viajar	hablar	aprender	resistir	llamar	responder
_____	_____	_____	_____	_____	_____

echar

_____

nosotros

trabajar	comprar	amar	vender	beber	correr
_____	_____	_____	_____	_____	_____

vivir

_____

tú y él

estudiar	comer	abrir	tomar	viajar	subir
_____	_____	_____	_____	_____	_____

pasar

_____

Uds.

trabajar	comprar	hablar	aprender	temer	escribir
_____	_____	_____	_____	_____	_____

viajar

_____

ellos

guardar	comprender	asistir	abrir	pasar	echar
————	————	————	————	————	————

beber

————

Aplicación

A. Write the following infinitives in the preterit and in the person indicated by the subject.

1. yo (llevar) ————————————

2. nosotros (abrir) ————————————

3. tú (llegar) ————————————

4. Pepe y Juan (comer) ————————————

5. ella (beber) ————————————

6. tú y él (meter) ————————————

7. María y Elena (viajar) ————————————

8. Ud. (vivir) ————————————

9. mis amigos (pasar) ————————————

10. Uds. (vender) ————————————

11. yo (abrir) ————————————

12. Pablo (asistir) ————————————

13. ellos (recibir) ————————————

14. nosotras (tomar) ————————————

15. vosotros (temer) ————————————

16. ella (abrir) ————————————

17. Juan y él (escribir) ————————————

18. Uds. (necesitar) ————————————

B. Write (1) the preterit and (2) the imperfect of each verb given in the present.

1. tomamos ————————————

2. enseñan ————————————

3. Ud. contesta ————————————

4. reciben ————————————

5. aprende ————————————

6. asisto ————————————

7. tememos ————————————

8. venden ————————————

9. aprendo ————————————

10. contesto ————————————

11. Uds. toman ————————————

12. abre ————————————

13. necesita ————————————

14. recibes ————————————

15. trabaja ————————————

16. echan ————————————

17. suben ————————————

18. comprendo ————————————

A. Write the following infinitives in the preterit and in the person indicated by the subject. (*continued*)

19. tú (vender) _____

20. nosotros (beber) _____

21. ellos (aprender) _____

22. yo (tomar) _____

23. ella (estudiar) _____

24. Ud. (beber) _____

25. yo (recibir) _____

B. Write (1) the preterit and (2) the imperfect of each verb given in the present. (*continued*)

19. corre _____

20. trabajo _____

21. Ud. prepara _____

22. guardan _____

23. pasamos _____

24. viajo _____

25. echas _____

Mastery Test

Write in the preterit, using infinitives on page 6.

1. we answered _____

2. they sold _____

3. I learned _____

4. did you (s., fam.) listen? _____

_____

5. she did not ask _____

6. you (s., for.) hid _____

7. we took _____

8. they did not drink _____

9. we attended _____

10. I did teach _____

11. you (s., fam.) asked _____

12. they worked _____

13. you (pl., for.) joined _____

14. I lived _____

15. you (pl., fam.) answered _____

_____

16. you (pl., for.) did write _____

_____

17. she understood _____

18. they did not learn _____

19. we wrote _____

20. did he study? _____

21. you (s., fam.) sold _____

22. he taught _____

23. he attended _____

24. I sold _____

25. you (pl., fam.) did live _____

_____

26. they received _____

27. I attended _____

28. they asked _____

29. we drank _____

30. you (s., for.) studied _____

31. I did not answer _____

32. did you (pl., for.) open? _____

_____

33. they did not understand _____

_____

34. you (s., fam.) did not need _____

_____

35. we sold _____

36. did you (s., for.) take? _____

_____

37. we did not receive _____

38. she feared _____

39. I wrote _____

40. did you (pl., fam.) ask? _____

Repaso (Present, imperfect, preterit)

Write in Spanish, using the infinitives below and on page 6.

echar to throw
viajar to travel
pasar to pass, spend
guardar to keep

preparar to prepare
responder to reply, respond
correr to run
subir to go up

1. they used to live _____

2. I was opening _____

3. they did work _____

4. we were going up _____

5. I understand _____

6. they did not take _____

7. he was running _____

8. they answered _____

9. I work _____

10. you (s., fam.) prepared _____

_____

11. you (pl., for.) used to study _____

_____

12. they keep _____

13. we were spending _____

14. I traveled _____

15. you (s., for.) need _____

16. I was not living _____

17. you (pl., for.) used to open _____

_____

18. he used to write _____

19. I go up _____

20. he did understand _____

21. I was writing _____

22. you (s., fam.) respond _____

23. we understood _____

24. you (pl., fam.) did not learn _____

_____

25. they are preparing _____

26. we learn _____

27. we ran _____

28. you (pl., for.) were spending _____

_____

29. they did work _____

30. we attend _____

31. we were not writing _____

32. I threw _____

33. we were studying _____

34. I worked _____

35. we were living _____

36. we kept _____

37. you (s., fam.) understood _____

_____

38. they attended _____

39. we used to sell _____

40. I am spending _____

41. I lived _____

42. you (s., fam.) fear _____

43. she listened _____

44. you (pl., fam.) did not keep _____

_____

45. he is drinking _____

46. they used to keep _____

47. he left _____

48. you (s., for.) feared _____

49. we went up _____

50. I do not answer _____

Future

The future of regular verbs is formed by adding the future endings to the full infinitive or, in some irregular verbs, to a modified form of the infinitive.

	1 **hablar**	*2* **comer**	*3* **partir**
yo	hablar *é* I will speak	comer *é* I will eat	partir *é* I will leave
tú	hablar *ás*		partir *ás*
Ud.	hablar *á*	comer *ás*	partir *á*
él(ella)	hablar *á*	comer *á*	partir *á*
nosotros	hablar *emos*	comer *á*	partir *emos*
vosotros	hablar *éis*	comer *emos*	partir *éis*
Uds.	hablar *án*	comer *éis*	partir *án*
ellos	hablar *án*	comer *án*	partir *án*
		comer *án*	

Note: Future endings are the same for all three conjugations of verbs. All forms of the future except the first-person plural have a written accent.

Para practicar

Write the future form of each verb that corresponds to the subject indicated:

yo

comprar	hablar	leer	vivir	sentir	ser
_____	_____	_____	_____	_____	_____

asistir

_____

tú

estudiar	encontrar	correr	tomar	vender	conocer
_____	_____	_____	_____	_____	_____

partir

_____

Ud.

enseñar	perder	dormir	aprender	recibir	abrir
_____	_____	_____	_____	_____	_____

necesitar

_____

Juan

dudar	creer	amar	escribir	guardar	correr
_____	_____	_____	_____	_____	_____

subir

_____

nosotros

contestar	temer	preguntar	subir	viajar	aprender
_____	_____	_____	_____	_____	_____

vivir

_____

vosotros

preparar	echar	contestar	trabajar	viajar	responder
_____	_____	_____	_____	_____	_____

amar

_____

Uds.

comprar	leer	sentir	recibir	decidir	andar
_____	_____	_____	_____	_____	_____

pasar

_____

los niños

preparar	aprender	echar	viajar	contestar	correr
_____	_____	_____	_____	_____	_____

marchar

_____

Aplicación

A.   Change the infinitive to correspond to the person indicated by the subject. Make all verbs future.

1. él (hablar) _____

2. nosotros (estar) _____

3. ella (ser) _____

4. Uds. (encontrar) _____

5. Juan (leer) _____

6. yo (dudar) _____

7. nosotros (perder) _____

8. tú (enseñar) _____

9. vosotros (dormir) _____

10. Ud. (andar) _____

11. tú (decidir) _____

12. yo (comprar) _____

13. él (vivir) _____

14. Ud. (sentir) _____

15. María (beber) _____

16. vosotros (estudiar) _____

17. él (abrir) _____

18. tú (vender) _____

19. ellos (escuchar) _____

20. Uds. (aprender) _____

21. ella (necesitar) _____

22. Ud. (contestar) _____

23. nosotras (temer) _____

24. yo (tomar) _____

25. tú (recibir) _____

B.   Change all verbs to future and translate new form into English.

1. (ellos) vivían _____

2. abrí _____

_____

_____

3. subimos _____

_____

4. comprendías _____

_____

5. aprendimos _____

_____

6. (ellos) trabajaron _____

_____

7. Ud. corría _____

_____

8. (ellas) contestaban _____

_____

9. trabajé _____

_____

10. preparabais _____

_____

11. pasábamos _____

_____

12. viajo _____

_____

13. echabas _____

_____

14. partí _____

_____

15. abríais _____

_____

16. Uds. escribían _____

_____

17. subí _____

_____

18. (ella) comprendió _____

_____

19. corrimos _____

_____

20. Ud. contestó _____

_____

21. tomamos _____

_____

22. (ellos) enseñaron _____

_____

23. acababas _____

_____

24. (él) trabajaba _____

_____

25. escribí _____

_____

24

Mastery Test

Write in Spanish in the tense indicated by the English, using the infinitives below.

admirar to admire *llamar* to call *discutir* to discuss *ofender* to offend
adornar to adorn *limpiar* to clean *insistir* to insist *emprender* to undertake
molestar to bother *cubrir* to cover *decidir* to decide

1. you (s., fam.) will adorn _____
   _____

2. I was admiring _____

3. you (pl., fam.) will offend _____
   _____

4. he bothers _____

5. you (pl., for.) will discuss _____
   _____

6. I insisted _____

7. he will discuss _____

8. we will undertake _____

9. they will clean _____

10. you (pl., for.) are calling _____
    _____

11. I will admire _____

12. he adorned _____

13. you (s., fam.) bother _____
    _____

14. I will discuss _____

15. they insisted _____

16. they were covering _____

17. we will cover _____

18. we admired _____

19. you (pl., for.) undertook _____
    _____

20. we insist _____

21. they discussed _____

22. we will clean _____

23. he was cleaning _____

24. I decided _____

25. she is calling _____

26. we were offending _____

27. we will call _____

28. you (s., for.) did discuss _____
    _____

29. we will not admire _____

30. they do not call _____

31. you (pl., fam.) are deciding _____

_____

32. I covered _____

33. you (s., for.) will not discuss _____

_____

34. we will not decide _____

35. will you (s., fam.) clean? _____

_____

36. you (pl., fam.) will not insist _____

_____

37. they will cover _____

38. you (pl., for.) cleaned _____

_____

39. we were insisting _____

40. he offended _____

Conditional

The conditional is formed adding the conditional endings to the full infinitive or, in some irregular verbs, to a modified form of the infinitive.

	1 hablar	*2* come	*3* partir
yo	hablar *ía* I should,	comer *ía* I should,	partir *ía* I should,
tú	hablar *ías* would speak,	comer *ías* would eat	partir *ías* would
Ud.	hablar *ía* etc.	comer *ía*	partir *ía* leave
él(ella)	hablar *ía*	comer *ía*	partir *ía*
nosotros	hablar *íamos*	comer *íamos*	partir *íamos*
vosotros	hablar *íais*	comer *íais*	partir *íais*
Uds.	hablar *ían*	comer *ían*	partir *ían*
ellos	hablar *ían*	comer *ían*	partir *ían*

Note: Conditional endings are identical to the *-er* and *-ir* imperfect endings, but are added to the full infinitive, not the stem. Conditional endings are the same for all conjugations.

All conditional forms must have a written accent.

Para practicar

Write the conditional form that corresponds to the subject indicated:

yo

admirar	decidir	trabajar	vivir	beber	abrir
_____	_____	_____	_____	_____	_____

morir

_____

tú

adornar	ofender	responder	estudiar	vender	escribir
_____	_____	_____	_____	_____	_____

sentir

_____

Ud.

molestar	emprender	correr	necesitar	aprender	llevar
_____	_____	_____	_____	_____	_____

partir

_____

él

llamar	echar	aprender	contestar	temer	sacar
_____	_____	_____	_____	_____	_____

hablar

_____

Luisa y yo

limpiar	viajar	comprender	preguntar	leer	tocar
_____	_____	_____	_____	_____	_____

comer

_____

tú y Juan

cubrir	pasar	subir	enseñar	creer	conocer
_____	_____	_____	_____	_____	_____

meter

_____

Uds.

discutir	guardar	abrir	escuchar	recibir	traer
_____	_____	_____	_____	_____	_____

pedir

_____

ellas

insistir	preparar	escribir	tomar	asistir	dormir
_____	_____	_____	_____	_____	_____

rogar

_____

Aplicación

A. Change the infinitives to the conditional, according to the person of the subject.

1. ellas (admirar) _____

2. Ud. (discutir) _____

3. tú (cubrir) _____

4. yo (limpiar) _____

5. tú y Juan (vender) _____

6. él (preguntar) _____

7. él y ella (vender) _____

8. nostoros (estudiar) _____

9. mi amigo y yo (vivir) _____

10. María (temer) _____

11. Pepe (abrir) _____

12. ellas (tomar) _____

13. nosotras (escribir) _____

14. María y él (contestar) _____

_____

15. Uds. (temer) _____

B. a) Change from the future to the conditional and translate.

1. contestaremos _____

2. aprenderé _____

3. (ellos) escucharán _____

4. (él) leerá _____

5. esconderemos _____

6. escribiréis _____

7. (Uds.) estudiarán _____

8. venderé _____

9. (ella) enseñará _____

10. (ellas) comprenderán _____

b) Change from the imperfect to the conditional and translate.

1. (Uds.) vivían _____

2. (él) abría _____

3. (ellos) trabajaban _____

4. subíamos _____

16. tú (llevar) _____

17. yo (beber) _____

18. Ud. (aprender) _____

19. él (echar) _____

20. ellos (viajar) _____

21. vosotros (necesitar) _____

22. Uds. (escuchar) _____

23. nosotras (enseñar) _____

24. ellas (asistir) _____

25. tú (recibir) _____

5. (él) comprendía _____

6. aprendíais _____

7. (él) corría _____

8. preparabas _____

9. guardábamos _____

10. (ella) viajaba _____

Mastery Test

Write in Spanish to correspond to the English tense and person.

1. you (s., fam.) will decide _____
_____

2. I should bother _____

3. you (s., for.) were adorning _____
_____

4. would he offend? _____

5. I insisted _____

6. we would discuss _____

7. they admired _____

8. he would not adorn _____

9. I will offend _____

10. they were offending _____

11. would she clean? _____

12. they undertake _____

13. they would admire _____

14. I will clean _____

15. you (pl., for.) would bother _____
_____

16. we will not cover _____

17. he covers _____

18. they would decide _____

19. will you (s., fam.) admire? _____

_____

20. we admired _____

21. they were insisting _____

22. I would not insist _____

23. you (pl., for.) cleaned _____

_____

24. she would decide _____

25. you (s., fam.) will insist _____

_____

26. would they call? _____

27. you (pl., fam.) would cover _____

_____

28. we will bother _____

29. they would not offend _____

_____

30. will I decide? _____

Progressive Tenses

Progressive tenses are compound tenses consisting of the appropriate tenses of *estar* and the present participle.

Present Participle: The present participle is formed by adding the ending *-ando* or *-iendo* to the infinitive stem.

	1	*2*	*3*
	hablar	**comer**	**partir**
	habl *ando* speaking	com *iendo* eating	part *iendo* leaving

Note: The present participle has only one form; it does not distinguish person or number.

Estar to be (in a state or condition) (see page 104 for complete verb).

Present Progressive: The present progressive is formed with the present tense of *estar* plus the present participle. It is used to describe action thought of as in *progress*.

yo	*estoy*	*hablando*, com*iendo*, part*iendo*	I am (in the act of) speaking, eating,
tú	*estás*	habl*ando*, com*iendo*, part*iendo*	leaving
Ud.	*está*	habl*ando*, com*iendo*, part*iendo*	you were speaking, eating, leaving.
él(ella)	*está*	habl*ando*, com*iendo*, part*iendo*	
nosotros	*estamos*	habl*ando*, com*iendo*, part*iendo*	
vosotros	*estáis*	habl*ando*, com*iendo*, part*iendo*	
Uds.	*están*	habl*ando*, com*iendo*, part*iendo*	
ellos	*están*	habl*ando*, com*iendo*, part*iendo*	

Past Progressive: The past progressive is formed with the imperfect tense of *estar* pluš he present participle. It describes action which *was* in progress at a given moment in the past.

yo	*estaba*	habl*ando*, com*iendo*, part*iendo*	I was (in the act of) speaking, eating,
tú	*estabas*	habl*ando*, com*iendo*, part*iendo*	leaving
Ud.	*estaba*	habl*ando*, com*iendo*, part*iendo*	you were speaking, etc.
él(ella)	*estaba*	habl*ando*, com*iendo*, part*iendo*	
nosotros	*estábamos*	habl*ando*, com*iendo*, part*iendo*	
vosotros	*estabais*	habl*ando*, com*iendo*, part*iendo*	
Uds.	*estaban*	habl*ando*, com*iendo*, part*iendo*	
ellos	*estaban*	habl*ando*, com*iendo*, part*iendo*	

Note: The present and past progressive tenses are used to express present or past (imperfect) action when that action is thought of as *continuing* or *in progress*. They are thus a more vivid, dramatic substitute for the present and imperfect, respectively. The *estar* verb indicates the person and number of the subject; the participle *always* remains the same.

Para practicar

Write the present participles of the following infinitives:

admirar	adornar	subir	cubrir	acabar	correr
_____	_____	_____	_____	_____	_____

responder	tomar	sacar	decidir	dar
_____	_____	_____	_____	_____

Write the present progressive form that corresponds to the subject:

yo

abrir	llevar	perder	buscar	estudiar	beber
_____	_____	_____	_____	_____	_____

tú

vivir	aprender	tomar	escribir	trabajar	enseñar
_____	_____	_____	_____	_____	_____

Uds.

vender	abrir	contestar	asistir	escuchar	entrar
_____	_____	_____	_____	_____	_____

nosotros

recibir	echar	admirar	pasar	responder	correr
_____	_____	_____	_____	_____	_____

Aplicación

A. Write the past progressive form for the subject indicated.

1. Juan (llevar) _____

2. tú (estudiar) _____

3. vosotros (trabajar) _____

B. Change the present and imperfect verbs so that they express action in progress, keeping original subject.

1. reciben _____

2. trabajábamos _____

3. abrís _____

4. Pepe y yo (subir) _____

5. ellas (correr) _____

6. mi amigo (escuchar) _____

_____

7. los niños (jugar) _____

8. nosotros (escribir) _____

9. tú (comer) _____

10. ella (partir) _____

11. ella y yo (tomar) _____

12. él y ella (acabar) _____

13. yo (responder) _____

14. ellos (decidir) _____

15. él (cubrir) _____

4. preguntabais _____

5. no escuchaba _____

6. vivimos _____

7. bebe _____

8. Uds. asistían _____

9. vendes _____

10. Ud. no tomaba _____

11. enseñaba _____

12. contestáis _____

13. Ud. estudia _____

14. no comía _____

15. aprendo _____

Mastery Test

Express each English verb two ways:

1. I was admiring _____ _____

2. you (s., fam.) are deciding _____ _____

3. he was cleaning _____ _____

4. they were insisting _____ _____

5. they are not preparing _____ _____

6. you (s., for.) are calling _____ _____

7. they were covering _____ _____

8. were you (pl., for.) adorning? _____ _____

9. he is drinking   _____   _____

10. we were living   _____   _____

11. you (s., fam.) were not writing   _____   _____

12. I am spending   _____   _____

13. they are studying   _____   _____

14. we were spending   _____   _____

15. are you (pl., fam.) going up?   _____   _____

16. I was opening   _____   _____

17. was he running?   _____   _____

18. I was not living   _____   _____

19. we are not writing   _____   _____

Repaso (Future, conditional, progressive)

Write in Spanish:

1. you (pl., for.) will attend _____

2. I was admiring _____

3. you (s., fam.) will offend _____

4. I should bother _____

5. you (pl., fam.) are looking for _____

6. you (s., for.) would not discuss _____

7. I was insisting _____

8. she is studying _____

9. I will go up _____

10. he would admire _____

11. they were responding _____

12. he is not bothering _____

13. will they discuss? _____

14. he was working _____

15. you (s., fam.) are not running _____

_____

16. he will listen _____

17. she was entering _____

18. we are spending _____

19. we would cover _____

20. they were cleaning _____

21. I will not open _____

22. you (pl., fam.) would lose _____

_____

23. you (s., for.) are calling _____

_____

24. he will clean _____

25. you (s., fam.) will teach _____

_____

26. you (pl., fam.) are working _____

_____

27. he will throw _____

28. I was writing _____

29. they are drinking _____

30. she would admire _____

31. we were calling _____

32. he was discussing _____

33. I will admire _____

34. you (s., for.) would bother _____

_____

35. they will spend _____

36. you (pl., for.) would write _____

_____

37. they were deciding _____

38. he will respond _____

Perfect Tenses

The perfect tenses are compound tenses, consisting in all cases of a form of the verb *haber* plus the past participle.

Present Participle: The past participle of regular verbs is formed by adding *-ado* or *-ido* to the stem.

1	*2*	*3*
hablar	**comer**	**partir**
habl *ado* spoken	com *ido* eaten	part *ido* left

The past participles does not change its ending to correspond to person and number in the perfect tenses.

Haber: *to have* is an irregular verb (see pages 104−5) which is used only in idiomatic expressions and as part of the perfect tenses.

Present Perfect: The present perfect is formed with the present tense of *haber* plus the past participle.

yo	*he* habl*ado* I have spoken	*he* com*ido* I have eaten	*he* part*ido* I have left
tú	*has* habl*ado*	*has* com*ido*	*has* part*ido*
Ud.	*ha* habl*ado*	*ha* com*ido*	*ha* part*ido*
él(ella)	*ha* habl*ado*	*ha* com*ido*	*ha* part*ido*
nosotros	*hemos* habl*ado*	*hemos* com*ido*	*hemos* part*ido*
vosotros	*habéis* habl*ado*	*habéis* com*ido*	*habéis* part*ido*
Uds.	*han* habl*ado*	*han* com*ido*	*han* part*ido*
ellos	*han* habl*ado*	*han* com*ido*	*han* part*ido*

Note: The same form of *haber* is used with all three conjugations. Negatives are formed by placing *no* before the *haber* verb.

Pluperfect: The pluperfect (past perfect) is formed with the imperfect of *haber* plus the past participle.

yo *había* hablado	I had spoken
había comido	I had eaten
había partido	I had left

The imperfect of *haber* is formed regularly (see page 8). What are the other forms of the pluperfect of *hablar*?

_____   _____   _____   _____   _____   _____

_____

Future Perfect: The future perfect is formed with the future of *haber* and the past participle.

yo *habré* hablado   I will have spoken
habré comido   I will have eaten
habré partido   I will have left

The future of *haber* is formed by adding the future endings to the stem *habr-*. What are all the forms of the future perfect of *comer*?

_____   _____   _____   _____   _____   _____

_____   _____

What is the English translation of each of the preceding forms? _____

_____

_____

Conditional Perfect: The conditional perfect is formed with the conditional of *haber* and the past participle.

yo *habría* hablado, comido, partido   I would have spoken, eaten, left

The conditional of *haber* is formed by adding the conditional endings (see page 26) to the future stem *habr-*. What are all the forms of the conditional perfect of *partir*?

_____   _____   _____   _____   _____   _____

_____   _____

What are the English translations?_____

_____

Para practicar

Write the infinitives in (1) the present perfect, (2) pluperfect, (3) future perfect, and (4) conditional perfect, in the subject indicated:

1. yo (aprender)   _____   _____   _____   _____

2. ellos (limpiar)   _____   _____   _____   _____

3. él (vivir)   _____   _____   _____   _____

4. nosotros (comprar) _____   _____   _____   _____

5. tú (asistir) _____ _____ _____ _____

6. ellos (vender) _____ _____ _____ _____

7. nosotros (tomar) _____ _____ _____ _____

8. él (aprender) _____ _____ _____ _____

9. Ud. (beber) _____ _____ _____ _____

10. ella (contestar) _____ _____ _____ _____

11. vosotros (recibir) _____ _____ _____ _____

12. ellos (preparar) _____ _____ _____ _____

13. nosotros (enseñar) _____ _____ _____ _____

14. tú (temer) _____ _____ _____ _____

15. Ud. (preguntar) _____ _____ _____ _____

16. Uds. (estudiar) _____ _____ _____ _____

17. él (pasar) _____ _____ _____ _____

18. nosotros (subir) _____ _____ _____ _____

19. Uds. (salir) _____ _____ _____ _____

20. tú (guardar) _____ _____ _____ _____

21. yo (esperar) _____ _____ _____ _____

22. vosotros (trabajar) _____ _____ _____ _____

23. ellos (vivir) _____ _____ _____ _____

24. Ud. (partir) _____ _____ _____ _____

25. ella (acabar) _____ _____ _____ _____

Aplicación

Change each simple tense verb to the corresponding perfect tense. Example: *como   he comido*; *hablé*
or *hablaba   había hablado*; *tomaré   habré tomado*; *partirías   habrías partido*

1. Ud. comprende _____

2. vendías _____

3. escucharon _____

4. subirán _____

5. pregunta _____

6. Ud. discutirá _____

7. aprendían _____

8. Ud. estudió _____

9. escribes _____

10. guardaremos _____

11. admirarían _____

12. echaréis _____

13. temiste _____

14. asisto _____

15. tomábamos _____

16. prepararías _____

17. bebió _____

18. viviremos _____

19. corremos _____

20. viajará _____

21. decidirías _____

22. contestabais _____

23. partisteis _____

24. limpiaré _____

25. molestaríais _____

Mastery Test

Translate into Spanish:

1. I will have learned _____

2. he had cleaned _____

3. we have bought _____

4. they had lived _____

5. he would have run _____

6. I have asked _____

7. you (s., fam.) will have received _____

_____

8. you (s., fam.) had feared _____

_____

9. he has attended _____

10. they would have sold _____

11. we will have taken _____

12. you (s., for.) have answered _____

_____

13. I have needed _____

_____

14. you (pl., for.) would have asked _____

_____

15. they have spent _____

16. you (s., fam.) will have discussed _____

_____

17. they have received _____

18. he would have decided _____

_____

19. they will have listened _____

_____

20. we will have entered _____

21. you (s., for.) would have attended _____

_____

22. you (pl., fam.) had understood _____

_____

23. we have lived _____

24. you (pl., for.) will have worked _____

_____

25. he had taken _____

Repaso (Indicative tenses)

Translate into Spanish:

1. you (s., fam.) answer _____

_____

2. they used to live _____

3. I was opening _____

4. you (pl., fam.) are selling _____

_____

5. I will admire _____

6. they did work _____

7. he asks _____

8. you (pl., for.) will not offend _____

_____

9. we were going up _____

10. they do not sell _____

11. I should bother _____

12. I was understanding _____

13. we study _____

14. are you (pl., fam.) adorning? _____

_____

15. you (pl., for.) were learning _____

_____

16. we do not live _____

17. you (s., for.) discuss _____

18. he was running _____

19. does she need? _____

20. they bothered _____

21. they did not answer _____

22. she fears _____

23. we insisted _____

24. I did work _____

25. I will throw _____

26. you (pl., fam.) used to prepare _____

_____

27. he opens _____

28. you (s., for.) were admiring _____

_____

29. they kept _____

30. I will offend _____

31. we were spending _____

32. he would adorn _____

33. we will clean _____

34. we write _____

35. they were covering _____

36. you (pl., for.) were throwing _____

_____

37. they will fear _____

38. I was living _____

39. I used to travel _____

40. you (s., fam.) study _____

41. you (pl., for.) are calling _____

_____

42. you (pl., fam.) would open _____

_____

43. I drink _____

44. we were insisting _____

45. you (s., fam.) used to write _____

_____

46. will they call? _____

47. I went up _____

48. they would not discuss _____

_____

49. he did understand _____

50. they live _____

Present Subjunctive

Present: The present subjunctive of regular verbs is formed in the same way as the present indicative, except that *-ar* verbs use the endings of *-er* verbs, and *-er* and *-ir* verbs use *-ar* endings. All endings are added to the stem.

		1	*2*	*3*
		hablar	**comer**	**partir**
yo	habl *e*	I may speak	com *a* I may eat	part *a* I may leave
tú	habl *es*	you may speak	com *as* you may eat	part *as* you may leave
Ud.	habl *e*	you may speak, etc.	com *a* you may eat	part *a*
él(ella)	habl *e*		com *a*	part *a*
nosotros	habl *emos*		com *amos*	part *amos*
vosotros	habl *éis*		com *áis*	part *áis*
Uds.	habl *en*		com *an*	part *an*
ellos	habl *en*		com *an*	part *an*

Note: The present subjunctive is also used for all negative commands, and affirmative commands with subjects *Ud.* and *Uds.* Thus: *coma*   you (he, she) may eat, or eat (Ud.)! *no partas* is *you may not leave* or *do not leave*. In addition, the first-person plural may be translated *let us* . . . . . . or *we may* . . . . . . All of these variations will be found in the drill materials.

Para practicar

Write the present subjunctive form that corresponds to the subject indicated:

yo

echar	aprender	molestar	emprender	comprender	asistir
_____	_____	_____	_____	_____	_____

vivir

_____

tú

viajar	comprender	llamar	estudiar	beber	abrir
_____	_____	_____	_____	_____	_____

escribir

_____

Ud.

pasar	subir	limpiar	necesitar	vender	escribir
___	___	___	___	___	___

preparar

___

ella

guardar	abrir	cubrir	contestar	aprender	llamar
___	___	___	___	___	___

tomar

___

nosotros

preparar	escribir	discutir	preguntar	temer	trabajar
___	___	___	___	___	___

unir

___

vosotros

trabajar	vivir	insistir	enseñar	leer	pasar
___	___	___	___	___	___

temer

___

Uds.

responder	admirar	decidir	escuchar	vivir	guardar
___	___	___	___	___	___

viajar

___

las chicas

correr   adornar   ofender   tomar   recibir   echar

_____   _____   _____   _____   _____   _____

subir

_____

Aplicación

Change from present indicative to present subjunctive.

1. lleva _____

2. vive _____

3. escriben _____

4. trabajáis _____

5. leen _____

6. hablo _____

7. Ud. estudia _____

8. llamamos _____

9. viajas _____

10. abre _____

11. creemos _____

12. manda _____

13. escribes _____

14. tomamos _____

15. comprenden _____

16. como _____

17. vives _____

18. asisto _____

19. Ud. nota _____

20. caminan _____

21. mete _____

22. observáis _____

23. partís _____

24. andas _____

25. insistimos _____

Mastery Test

Translate into Spanish:

1. I may not understand _____

_____

2. run! _____

3. he may ask _____

4. I may study _____

5. they may drink _____

6. he may sell _____

7. they may study _____

8. I may not sell _____

9. drink! _____

10. we may understand _____

11. I may receive _____

12. they may sell _____

13. you (pl., fam.) may study _____

_____

14. do (s., fam.) not ask! _____

15. we may not run _____

16. you (s., fam.) may receive _____

_____

17. I may teach _____

18. you (pl., fam.) may understand _____

_____

19. let us call _____

20. I may open _____

21. write! _____

22. she may travel _____

23. you (s., fam.) may take _____

_____

24. you (s., for.) may live _____

_____

25. let us insist _____

Imperfect Subjunctive

The imperfect subjunctive is formed by adding either the *-ra* or the *-se* endings, which are listed below, to the stem of the third-person plural preterit indicative.

	1	*2*	*3*
	hablar	**comer**	**partir**
	habla ron	*comie* ron	*partie* ron

-ra endings

yo	habla *ra* I might speak	comie *ra* I might eat	partie *ra* I might leave
tú	habla *ras*	comie *ras*	partie *ras*
Ud.	habla *ra*	comie *ra*	partie *ra*
él(ella)	habla *ra*	comie *ra*	partie *ra*
nosotros	hablá *ramos*	comié *ramos*	partié *ramos*
vosotros	habla *rais*	comie *rais*	partie *rais*
Uds.	habla *ran*	comie *ran*	partie *ran*
ellos	habla *ran*	comie *ran*	partie *ran*

-se endings

yo	habla *se* I might speak	comie *se* I might eat	partie *se* I might leave
tú	habla *ses*	comie *ses*	partie *ses*
Ud.	habla *se*	comie *se*	partie *se*
él(ella)	habla *se*	comie *se*	partie *se*
nosotros	hablá *semos*	comié *semos*	partié *semos*
vosotros	habla *seis*	comie *seis*	partie *seis*
Uds.	habla *sen*	comie *sen*	partie *sen*
ellos	habla *sen*	comie *sen*	partie *sen*

Note: The first-person plural of both *-ra* and *-se* imperfect subjunctives must have a written accent. There is no difference in meaning between the two forms of the imperfect subjunctive and they may be used interchangeably, although the *-ra* form is the more common.

Para practicar

Write the *-ra* subjunctive form of the following infinitives according to the subject given.

yo

temer	asistir	abrir	acabar	escuchar	necesitar
_____	_____	_____	_____	_____	_____

Ud.

estudiar	abrir	aprender	tener	hablar	enseñar
_____	_____	_____	_____	_____	_____

nosotros

comprender	comer	entrar	partir	vivir	meter
_____	_____	_____	_____	_____	_____

Write these infinitives in the *-se* subjunctive that corresponds to the subject given.

tú

partir	preguntar	vivir	vender	hablar	guardar
_____	_____	_____	_____	_____	_____

ella

enseñar	tomar	comer	aprender	asistir	pasar
_____	_____	_____	_____	_____	_____

Uds.

hablar	contestar	estudiar	tomar	leer	escribir
_____	_____	_____	_____	_____	_____

Aplicación

A. Write the imperfect subjunctive of the infinitive in the person indicated.

1. él (hablar) _____

2. Elena y yo (vivir) _____

3. nosotros (correr) _____

4. tú (partir) _____

5. yo (pasar) _____

6. vosotros (esperar) _____

7. Uds. (acabar) _____

8. Ud. (caminar) _____

9. él (comprender) _____

10. Juan y Pedro (tomar) _____

B. Change from present to imperfect subjunctive.

1. contestemos _____

2. vendas _____

3. pregunte _____

4. aprenda _____

5. escuchen _____

6. Ud. escriba _____

7. aprendan _____

8. Ud. estudie _____

9. vivamos _____

10. tema _____

A. Write the imperfect subjunctive of the infinitive in the person indicated. (*continued*)

11. yo (escribir) _____

12. Ud. (amar) _____

13. tú (beber) _____

14. nosotros (comprar) _____

15. ellos (subir) _____

B. Change from present to imperfect subjunctive. (*continued*)

11. abra _____

12. enseñen _____

13. asista _____

14. tomemos _____

15. Uds. reciban _____

Mastery Test

Translate into Spanish:

1. I might teach _____

2. they might live _____

3. we might go up _____

4. I might not understand _____

_____

5. they might take _____

6. he might run _____

7. you (s., fam.) might answer _____

_____

8. I might work _____

9. you (pl., fam.) might not prepare _____

_____

10. you (s., for.) might study _____

_____

11. they might keep _____

12. we might not spend _____

13. I might travel _____

14. you (s., fam.) might need _____

_____

15. I might not live _____

16. you (pl. fam.) might open _____

_____

17. she might write _____

18. you (pl., for.) might respond _____

_____

19. he might fear _____

20. they might eat _____

Perfect Tenses of the Subjunctive

Present Perfect Subjunctive

The *present perfect subjunctive* is formed from the *present* subjunctive of *haber* plus the past participle. Present subjunctive of *haber* is found on page 104.

	1 **hablar**	*2* **comer**	*3* **partir**
yo	*haya* hablado	*haya* comido	*haya* partido
tú	*hayas* hablado	*hayas* comido	*hayas* partido
Ud.	*haya* hablado	*haya* comido	*haya* partido
él(ella)	*haya* hablado	*haya* comido	*haya* partido
nosotros	*hayamos* hablado	*hayamos* comido	*hayamos* partido
vosotros	*hayáis* hablado	*hayáis* comido	*hayáis* partido
Uds.	*hayan* hablado	*hayan* comido	*hayan* partido
ellos	*hayan* hablado	*hayan* comido	*hayan* partido
	(I, you, he, etc., may have spoken)	(I, you, he, etc., may have eaten)	(I, you, he, etc., may have left)

Note: As with other perfect tenses, the past participle does not change. The person and number of the verb form is indicated only by the *haber* verb.

Second person plural forms must have a written accent.

The negative is formed by placing *no* before the *haber* verb.

Pluperfect Subjunctive

The pluperfect subjunctive is formed from the imperfect (*-ra* or *-se*) subjunctive of *haber* plus the past participle. Imperfect subjunctive of *haber* is found on page 105.

	1	*2*	*3*
yo	*hubiera (hubiese)* hablado	*hubiera (hubiese)* comido	*hubiera (hubiese)* partido
tú	*hubieras* hablado	*hubieras* comido	*hubieras* partido
Ud.	*hubiera* hablado	*hubiera* comido	*hubiera* partido
él(ella)	*hubiera* hablado	*hubiera* comido	*hubiera* partido
nosotros	*hubiéramos* hablado	*hubiéramos* comido	*hubiéramos* partido
vosotros	*hubierais* hablado	*hubierais* comido	*hubierais* partido
Uds.	*hubieran* hablado	*hubieran* comido	*hubieran* partido
ellos	*hubieran* hablado	*hubieran* comido	*hubieran* partido
	(I, you, he, etc., might have spoken)	(I, you, he, etc., might have eaten)	(I, you, he, etc., might have left)

Para practicar

Write the *present perfect subjunctive* in the person indicated:

yo (estudiar) _____

María (necesitar) _____

Ud. (viajar) _____

nosotros (pasar) _____

tú (tomar) _____

ellos (vender) _____

tu amigo y tú (asistir) _____

Uds. (llamar) _____

Write in the *pluperfect subjunctive*:

yo (vivir) _____

Uds. (guardar) _____

tú (caminar) _____

ellos (beber) _____

nosotros (echar) _____

vosotros (asistir) _____

Ud. (aprender) _____

Aplicación

Change from simple to corresponding compound tense in the subjunctive. Example: *coma—haya comido*; *hablásemos—hubiéramos hablado*.

1. escuche _____

2. viviéramos _____

3. guardasen _____

4. trabajen _____

5. comoprendamos _____

6. viviésemos _____

7. subieras _____

8. comprenda _____

9. no tomase _____

10. Ud. corra _____

11. respondieran _____

12. prepares _____

13. estudiarais _____

14. pasemos _____

15. viajéis _____

16. Uds. necesiten _____

17. suba _____

18. partiera _____

19. no aprendas _____

20. no conteste _____

21. temieras _____

22. asistiesen _____

23. no viva _____   25. llaméis _____ —

24. discutieses _____

Mastery Test

Translate into Spanish:

1. I may have learned _____

2. he might have taken _____

3. she might have cleaned _____

4. you (s., fam.) may have worked _____

5. we may have bought _____

6. we might have lived _____

7. they might have received _____

8. you (pl., fam.) might have understood _____

9. she might have attended _____

10. we may have taken _____

11. I may have needed _____

12. you (s., for.) might have asked _____

13. they may have lived _____

14. she might have run _____

15. we may have entered _____

16. I might have asked _____

17. they may have listened _____

18. you (pl., fam.) may have feared _____

19. she may have decided _____

20. you (pl., for.) might have answered _____

Repaso del subjuntivo

Write in Spanish:

1. I may understand

_____

2. you (pl., fam.) may have drunk

_____

3. we might have understood

_____

4. I may not receive

_____

5. I might teach

_____

6. we might run

_____

7. you (s., for.) might have received

_____

8. you (s., fam.) may understand

_____

9. we might not understand

_____

10. I may have studied

_____

11. I might not run

_____

12. we may have taught

_____

13. they may have sold

_____

14. they might have drunk

_____

15. I may not have received

_____

16. she might have received

_____

17. let us understand

_____

18. he may have drunk

_____

19. study! (s., for.)

_____

20. we might have received

_____

21. I may sell

_____

22. they might understand

_____

23. we may have studied

_____

24. you (pl., fam.) may not study

_____

25. I might study

_____

26. I may have asked

_____

27. you (s., fam.) may have sold

_____

28. you (pl., fam.) might have drunk

_____

29. I might not have taught

_____

30. we may study

_____

31. do not sell! (pl., fam.)

_____

32. I might understand

_____

33. she may have studied

_____

34. he might have drunk

_____

35. they might have taught

_____

36. let's not ask

_____

37. they might drink

_____

38. run! (pl.)

_____

39. they might run

_____

40. you (pl., for.) may have studied

_____

Reflexive Verbs

Reflexive verbs are verbs in which the object *reflects* the subject, that is, the subject does the action to itself. Therefore, in Spanish reflexive verbs, the object pronoun must change each time the person of the subject changes. The reflexive verb has the same forms as a nonreflexive verb, but the object pronoun is always included, in the same person as the ending of the verb indicates.

Present of Reflexive Verbs: levantar(se) to get (oneself) up, to arise

yo	*me* levanto	I get (myself) up
tú	*te* levantas	you get (yourself) up
Ud.	*se* levanta	
él(ella)	*se* levanta	

nosotros *nos* levantamos

vostros *os* levantáis

Uds. *se* levantan

ellos *se* levantan

Reflexive pronouns are the same for verbs of all three conjugations. The infinitive indicates that the verb is reflexive by having *-se* attached to it (*levantarse*). The *se* is removed with the infinitive ending when the personal endings are attached. The reflexive is also the same form for all tenses of the verb.

Imperfect: *yo me levantaba* I was getting up. Write the other forms of the imperfect, taking care to use the correct reflexive pronoun with each form (Imperfect, p. 8):

_____ _____ _____ _____

_____ _____ _____ _____

Preterit: *yo me levanté* I got up. Write the other forms of the preterit (p. 13):

_____ _____ _____ _____

_____ _____ _____ _____

Future: *yo me levantaré* I shall get up. Write the other forms of the future (p. 20):

_____ _____ _____ _____

_____ _____ _____ _____

Conditional: *yo me levantaría* I would get up. Write the other forms of the conditional (p. 26):

_____ _____ _____ _____

_____ _____ _____ _____

Progressive Tenses: *yo me estoy levantando* or *yo estoy levantándome*   I am getting up.
   Note that the pronoun may either precede or follow in the progressive. Write the *yo* form of the *past* progressive in Spanish and translate into English:

yo _____   _____

Perfect Tenses: *Present*: *yo me he levantado*   I have gotten up. The pronoun precedes the *haber* verb in all perfect tenses. Change the present perfect to (1) pluperfect, (2) future perfect, and (3) conditional perfect, and translate each into English:

yo me he levantado: Translate:

(1) yo _____   (1) _____

(2) _____   (2) _____

(3) _____   (3) _____

Subjunctive: Present: *yo me levante*   I may get up. Write the other forms of present subjunctive:

_____   _____   _____   _____

_____   _____

Imperfect: *yo me levantara* (*me levantase*)   I might get up. Write the other forms of the imperfect subjunctive, first the *-ra* and then the *-se* forms:

tú _____   tú (-se) _____

Ud. _____   Ud. _____

él _____   él _____

_____   _____

_____   _____

_____   _____

Present Perfect: yo me haya levantado   I may have gotten up. Write the singular forms of the present perfect subjunctive and translate into English:

yo _____   Trans. _____

tú _____   _____

Ud. _____   _____

él _____   _____

Pluperfect: yo me hubiera levantado   I might have gotten up. Write the plural forms of the imperfect subjunctive (*-se* form) and translate into English:

nosotros _____   Trans. _____

vosotros _____   _____

Uds. _____   _____

ellos _____   _____

Aplicación

Two other verbs which are treated in a manner similar to *levantarse* are *lavarse* to wash, get washed, and *peinarse* to comb oneself, get combed.

A. Change the verbs so that they express the idea of a subject acting on itself:

1. lavéis _____

2. peinaban _____

3. levantó _____

4. peinemos _____

5. levantábamos _____

6. lavan _____

7. levantamos _____

8. hayan peinado _____

B. Change each simple tense to a corresponding compound tense, keeping the person of the original verb.

1. se levanten _____

2. nos levantamos _____

3. te peinas _____

4. os levantáis _____

5. nos peinaremos _____

6. me peiné _____

7. se levantaba _____

8. nos levantaríamos _____

9. lavabas _____

10. peiné _____

11. lavantáis _____

12. hubieras levantado _____

13. peina _____

14. lavaré _____

15. peinarías _____

9. se peinaron _____

10. se lave _____

11. os peinéis _____

12. nos lavemos _____

13. me levante _____

14. se levantarán _____

15. me lavaré _____

Mastery Test

Write in Spanish, using reflexive verbs:

1. he may have washed _____

2. they were washing _____

3. they comb their hair _____

4. he might wash _____

5. I had gotten up _____

6. they got up _____

7. they will have washed _____

8. I am combing my hair _____

9. they would have gotten up _____

10. I used to get up _____

11. I wash _____

12. he may get up _____

13. we shall wash _____

14. he has washed _____

15. we might comb our hair _____

16. they washed _____

17. I would wash _____

18. they get up _____

19. you (s., fam.) washed _____

20. they might have washed _____

Repaso de verbos regulares

A.   Change each verb to represent more than one person in the same tense.

1. acabo _____

16. habrías tomado _____

2. comprendiste _____

17. escucha _____

3. él temía _____

18. he estudiado _____

4. necesitaré _____

19. habrás temido _____

5. partirías _____

20. aprenderá _____

6. estoy enseñando _____

21. comprendas _____

7. partes _____

22. está viviendo _____

8. Ud. hable _____

23. Ud. había acabado _____

9. ha enseñado _____

24. contesté _____

10. hayas hablado _____

25. Ud. vendiese _____

11. estaba lavándose _____

26. yo habría partido _____

12. habías vendido _____

27. abrías _____

13. él hubiese asistido _____

28. Ud. entraría _____

14. bebieras _____

29. estabas comiendo _____

15. habrá preguntado _____

30. Ud. haya tomado _____

B. Translate into English:

1. parto _____

2. Uds. escribieron _____

3. asistiréis _____

4. ellos vivían _____

5. tomaríamos _____

6. enseñasteis _____

7. él está estudiando _____

8. temeremos _____

9. Ud. estaba abriendo _____
_____

10. ella vendería _____

11. has asistido _____

12. Ud. ha comido _____

13. ellos habían comprendido _____
_____

14. estás escuchando _____

15. habremos tenido _____

16. yo había estudiado _____

17. estaba levantándome _____
_____

18. habrás hablado _____

19. bebiéramos _____

20. Ud. habría contestado _____
_____

21. comas _____

22. él escriba _____

23. él se haya lavado _____

24. aprendiésemos _____

25. hubieras estudiado _____

26. hayáis hablado _____

27. Uds. hubieran comido _____
_____

28. ellos temen _____

29. Uds. habrían llevado _____
_____

30. Uds. llevaban _____

C. Write in Spanish:

1. they fear _____

2. she might have left _____

3. you (s., fam.) used to eat _____

4. we may have spoken _____

5. did you (pl., fam.) speak? _____

6. I used to leave _____

7. we will learn _____

8. you (s., fam.) might take _____

9. he would not write _____

10. they understood _____

11. you (s., fam.) are answering _____

12. they would have left _____

13. you (pl., fam.) were speaking _____

14. I have studied _____

15. do not finish! (pl., fam.) _____

16. they had left _____

17. I will have taught _____

18. you (s., for.) will have lived _____

19. we are living _____

20. you (pl., for.) would have taught _____

21. let us fear _____

22. you (s., fam.) do not read _____

23. he might sell _____

24. you (pl., fam.) may not have eaten _____

25. he was selling _____

26. you (pl., fam.) might not have listened _____

27. I sell _____

28. will you (s., fam.) read? _____

29. they used to carry _____

30. you (s., fam.) wrote _____

31. you (pl., fam.) will attend _____

32. we would take _____

33. she is not studying _____

34. you (pl., fam.) were opening _____

35. you (s., for.) have not attended _____

36. I had understood _____

37. you (s., fam.) would carry _____

38. they will have studied _____

39. you (pl., for.) would not have needed _____

40. drink! (pl., for.) _____

41. we might not attend _____

42. you (s., fam.) have lived _____

43. he may have finished _____

44. you (pl., for.) might have learned _____

45. do you (pl., fam.) open? _____

46. I used to fear _____

47. you (s., fam.) had taken _____

48. they asked _____

49. you (s., for.) will enter _____

50. would you (s., fam.) read? _____

Stem-Changing Verbs—Class I

Stem-changing verbs change the last vowel of the stem under certain conditions.

In stem-changing verbs of Class I (*-ar* or *-er* verbs), the *e* or *o* of the stem changes to *ie* or *ue*, respectively, in all the forms of both the present indicative and the present subjunctive, except the *nosotros* and *vosotros* forms.

Present Indicative:

	1		*2*	
	pensar to think		**entender** to understand	
yo	*piens* o I think, am thinking		*entiend* o I understand, etc.
tú	*piens* as		*entiend* es
Ud.	*piens* a		*entiend* e
él(ella)	*piens* a		*entiend* e
nosotros	pens amos		entend emos
vosotros	pens áis		entend éis
Uds.	*piens* an		*entiend* en
ellos	*piens* an		*entiend* en

Note: The stem is formed in the regular way when it is not accented. No other indicative tense except the present has an accented stem for regular verbs. The present is thus the only indicative tense in which this change occurs.

Present Subjunctive:

	1		*2*	
	contar to tell		**volver** to return	
yo	*cuent* e I may tell		*vuelv* a I may return
tú	*cuent* es		*vuelv* as
Ud.	*cuent* e		*vuelv* a
él(ella)	*cuent* e		*vuelv* a
nosotros	cont emos		volv amos
vosotros	cont éis		volv áis
Uds.	*cuent* en		*vuelv* an
ellos	*cuent* en		*vuelv* an

What would the present subjunctive of (1) *pensar* (2) *entender* be?

(1) _____ _____ _____ _____ _____ _____

_____ _____

(2) _____ _____ _____ _____ _____ _____

_____ _____

What would the present indicative of (1) *contar* and (2) *volver* be?

(1) _____ _____ _____ _____ _____ _____

_____ _____

(2) _____ _____ _____ _____ _____ _____

_____ _____

Other Verbs of Class I:

calentar to warm	*devolver* to give back, return	*confesar* to confess
cerrar to close	*encender* to burn, light	*costar* to cost
mostrar to show	*acertar* to succeed, guess right	*nevar** to snow
morder to bite	*acordar* to agree, remember	*llover** to rain
perder to lose	*acostar(se)* to put (go) to bed	*encontrar* to find, meet
mover to move	*aprobar* to approve	
revolver to stir, turnover	*sentar(se)* to seat (sit)	* This verb is used only in the third-person plural.

Para practicar

A. Write the infinitive in the *present indicative* in the subject indicated:

yo

cerrar	encontrar	mostrar	perder	revolver	encender
___	___	___	___	___	___

Uds.

confesar	acostarse	mover	devolver	acertar	acordar
___	___	___	___	___	___

nosotros

sentarse	contar	mostrar	perder	devolver	entender
_____	_____	_____	_____	_____	_____

B.   Write the infinitives in the *present subjunctive* in the subject indicated:

tú

contar	pensar	morder	aprobar	devolver	entender
_____	_____	_____	_____	_____	_____

ellas

cerrar	encontrar	mostrar	perder	mover	encender
_____	_____	_____	_____	_____	_____

vosotros

entender	revolver	mostrar	mover	confesar	acordar
_____	_____	_____	_____	_____	_____

Mastery Test

A. Translate into English:

1. se acuestan _____

2. acuerdo _____

3. ella vuelve _____

4. Ud. caliente _____

5. mostremos _____

6. perdéis _____

7. Uds. revuelvan _____

8. enciendas _____

9. él aprobó _____

10. me sentaba _____

11. costó _____

12. nevará _____

13. confieso _____

14. ellos devuelven _____

15. cierre Ud. _____

B. Translate into Spanish:

1. you (pl., fam.) lost _____

2. they may understand _____

_____

3. we may meet _____

4. do you (s., fam.) close? _____

_____

5. you (s., fam.) do not understand _____

_____

6. they moved _____

7. I was moving _____

8. they may show _____

9. you (s., fam.) move _____

10. we warmed _____

11. I am lighting _____

12. they do not lose _____

13. I may bite _____

14. you (s., fam.) may stir _____

_____

15. it costs _____

Stem-Changing Verbs—Class II

In stem-changing verbs of Class II (-*ir* verbs), the *e* or *o* of the stem changes to *ie* or *ue* respectively, in all the forms of the present indicative tense, except the *nosotros* and *vosotros* forms, and to *i* or *u* in the third-person singular and plural of the preterit. In the present subjunctive, the *ie* and *ue* change to *i* and *u*, respectively, in the *nosotros* and *vosotros* forms.

Present:

	sentir to feel	**dormir** to sleep
yo	*sient* o I feel, am feeling	*duerm* o I sleep, am sleeping
tú	*sient* es	*duerm* es
Ud.	*sient* e	*duerm* e
él(ella)	*sient* e	*duerm* e
nosotros	sent imos	dorm imos
vosotros	sent ís	dorm ís
Uds.	*sient* en	*duerm* en
ellos	*sient* en	*duerm* en

Present Participle: *sint* iendo   feeling   *durm* iendo   sleeping

Preterit:

yo	sent í I felt, did feel	dorm í I slept, did sleep
tú	sent iste	dorm iste
Ud.	*sint* ió	*durm* ió
él(ella)	*sint* ió	*durm* ió
nosotros	sent imos	dorm imos
vosotros	sent isteis	dorm isteis
Uds.	*sint* ieron	*durm* ieron
ellos	*sint* ieron	*durm* ieron

No other tenses of the indicative are affected.

Present Subjunctive:

yo	*sient* a I may feel	*duerm* a I may sleep
tú	*sient* as	*duerm* as
Ud.	*sient* a	*duerm* a
él(ella)	*sient* a	*duerm* a
nosotros	*sint* amos	*durm* amos
vosotros	*sint* áis	*durm* áis
Uds.	*sient* an	*duerm* an
ellos	*sient* an	*duerm* an

Imperfect Subjunctive: Since the imperfect subjunctive is formed from the stem of the third-person plural preterit, all forms reflect the same stem-change.

yo	*sint* iera	*sint* iese	I might	*durm* iera	*durm* iese	I might
tú	*sint* ieras	*sint* ieses	feel	*durm* ieras	*durm* ieses	sleep
Ud.	*sint* iera	*sint* iese		*durm* iera	*durm* iese
él(ella)	*sint* iera	*sint* iese		*durm* iera	*durm* iese
nosotros	*sint* iéramos	*sint* iésemos		*durm* iéramos	*durm* iésemos
vosotros	*sint* ierais	*sint* ieseis		*durm* ierais	*durm* ieseis
Uds.	*sint* ieran	*sint* iesen		*durm* ieran	*durm* iesen
ellos	*sint* ieran	*sint* iesen		*durm* ieran	*durm* iesen

Others:

advertir to notice	*mentir* to lie
consentir to consent	*morir* to die
divertir(se) to amuse (oneself), have fun	*herir* to wound

Para practicar

Change the infinitives to the tense and person indicated:

Present indicative   **tú**

advertir	mentir	morir	herir	consentir
_____	_____	_____	_____	_____

Present Subjunctive   **Ud.**

divertirse	sentir	dormir	mentir	morir
_____	_____	_____	_____	_____

Preterit   **ellos**

herir	advertir	divertirse	dormir	consentir
_____	_____	_____	_____	_____

Imperfect Subjunctive   **nosotros**

morir	sentir	mentir	dormir	advertir
_____	_____	_____	_____	_____

Present Participle

morir	herir	consentir	advertir	divertirse
_____	_____	_____	_____	_____

Mastery Test

A. Translate into English:

1. Ud. mentía _____

2. dormimos _____

3. ella murió _____

4. ellos mintieran _____

5. él había sentido _____

6. ellos se divierten _____

7. él hirió _____

8. él consienta _____

9. no advierto _____

10. Uds. mintieron _____

11. sentí _____

12. mueras _____

13. sintáis _____

14. ellos duerman _____

15. nos divirtamos _____

B. Translate into Spanish:

1. they do not wound _____

2. you (s., fam.) have slept _____

_____

3. we may consent _____

4. I might die _____

5. he may sleep _____

6. you (s., fam.) amused yourself _____

_____

7. we will lie _____

8. they were dying _____

9. he was feeling _____

10. he might sleep _____

11. I would consent _____

12. you (s., for.) noticed _____

13. I sleep _____

14. they might feel _____

15. you (pl., fam.) may amuse yourself _____

_____

Stem-Changing Verbs—Class III

In stem-changing verbs of Class III (-*ir* verbs), the *e* of the stem changes to *i* in all the forms of the present indicative tense, except the *nosotros* and *vosotros* forms, and in the third-person singular and plural of the preterit.

Pedir   to ask for

Present Indicative: *pido*, *pides*, *pide*, pedimos, pedís, *piden*   I ask for, etc.

Imperfect: pedía, etc.   I was looking for, etc.

Preterit: pedí, pediste, *pidió*, pedimos, pedisteis, *pidieron*   I asked for, etc.

Future: pediré, etc.   I will ask for, etc.

Conditional: pediría, etc.   I would ask for, etc.

Present Participle: *pidiendo*   asking for

Past Participle: pedido

Present Subjunctive: *pida*, *pidas*, *pida*, *pidamos*, *pidáis*, *pidan*   I may ask for, etc.

Imperfect Subjunctive: *pidiera* (*pidiese*), etc.   I might ask for, etc.

Present Perfect Subjunctive: haya pedido, etc.   I may have looked for, etc.

Pluperfect Subjunctive: hubiera (hubiese) pedido, etc.   I might have looked for, etc.

All Spanish forms not in italics are regular.

Others:	*gemir* to groan
impedir to prevent	*medir* to measure
repetir to repeat	*competir* to compete
servir to serve	
vestirse to get dressed, dress	

Para practicar

Change the infinitives to the tense and person indicated:

Present indicative   **Ud.**

impedir	competir	servir	medir
_____	_____	_____	_____

Present subjunctive   **vosotros**

gemir	pedir	impedir	competir
_____	_____	_____	_____

Preterit **ellos**

vestirse	servir	medir	impedir
_____	_____	_____	_____

Mastery Test

Translate into English:

1. ellos gimieran _____

2. me vista _____

3. él pediría _____

4. medíamos _____

5. midáis _____

6. impedimos _____

7. Ud. gimió _____

8. competiré _____

9. sirviéramos _____

10. él gime _____

11. mediste _____

12. sirvieron _____

13. compito _____

14. se visten _____

15. impidas _____

Repaso (Stem-changing verbs)

A. Write the *third-person singular present indicative* of the following infinitives:

ella

gemir	competir	cerrar	sentir	impedir	mostrar
_____	_____	_____	_____	_____	_____

encontrar	divertirse	sentarse	revolver
_____	_____	_____	_____

B. Write the *first-person plural present subjunctive* of the following infinitives:

nosotros

aprobar	medir	dormir	confesar	mentir	advertir
_____	_____	_____	_____	_____	_____

pedir	vestirse	repetir	consentir
_____	_____	_____	_____

C. Write in Spanish:

1. they understand _____

2. we may consent _____

3. I may dress _____

4. he is not amusing himself _____

_____

5. we may close _____

6. you (s., fam.) asked for _____

_____

7. she did not notice _____

8. he meets _____

9. you (s., for.) might groan _____

_____

10. I may die _____

11. you (s., fam.) may move _____

_____

12. we might serve _____

13. they notice _____

14. I close _____

15. he competes _____

16. you (s., fam.) may show _____

_____

17. I might amuse myself _____

_____

18. they served _____

19. you (pl., fam.) do not lose _____

_____

20. she may sleep _____

21. he prevents _____

22. I may give back _____

23. they felt _____

24. you (pl., for.) may prevent _____

_____

25. does he understand? _____

26. they are not dying _____

27. she did not compete _____

28. it may snow _____

29. you (s., fam.) are lying _____

_____

30. they might ask for _____

Orthographic Changes

Orthographic-changing verbs change the spelling of certain consonants when it is necessary to maintain a uniform pronunciation of their stems.

Verbs ending in -car change *c* to *qu* before the letter *e*.

Buscar to look for

Present Indicative: busco, etc. I look for, etc. (p. 1)

Imperfect: buscaba, etc. I was looking for, etc. (p. 8)

Preterit: *busqué*, buscaste, buscó, etc. I looked for, etc. (p. 13)

Future: buscaré, etc. I will look for, etc. (p. 20)

Conditional: buscaría, etc. I would look for, etc. (p. 26)

Present Participle: buscando looking for

Past Participle: buscado looked for

Present Subjunctive: *busque, busques, busque, busquemos, busquéis, busquen* I may look for, etc.

Imperfect Subjunctive: buscara (buscase), etc. I might look for, etc. (p. 46)

Present Perfect Subjunctive: haya buscado, etc. I may have looked for, etc. (p. 49)

Pluperfect Subjunctive: hubiera (hubiese) buscado, etc. I might have looked for, etc. (p. 49)

Verb forms not in italics are not affected.

Others:	*sacar* to take out
colocar to place	*secar* to dry
explicar to explain	*convocar* to call together
indicar to indicate	*replicar* to reply
marcar to mark	*pecar* to sin
mascar (masticar) to chew	
rascar to scratch	

Verbs ending in -gar change *g* to *gu* before the letter *e*. The *u* is not pronounced.

Pagar to pay

Present Indicative: pago, pagas, etc. I pay, etc.

Imperfect: pagaba, etc. I was paying, etc.

Preterit: *pagué*, pagaste, pagó, etc. I paid, etc.

Future: pagaré, etc. I will pay, etc.

Conditional: pagaría, etc. I would pay, etc.

Present Participle: pagando paying

Past Participle: pagado paid

Present Subjunctive: *pague, pagues, pague, paguemos, paguéis, paguen* I may pay, etc.

Imperfect Subjunctive: pagara (pagase) I might pay, etc.

Present Perfect Subjunctive: haya pagado, etc.   I may have paid, etc.

Pluperfect Subjunctive: hubiera (hubiese) pagado, etc.   I might have paid, etc.

Others:

apagar to turn off, extinguish	*llegar* to arrive
arriesgar to risk	*obligar* to oblige
cargar to load	*vagar* to wander
castigar to punish	*colgar** to hang up
ahogar to drown	*rogar** to beg, ask
entregar to hand over	*negar** to deny
fatigar to tire	*cegar** to blind

* see page 85

Verbs ending in *-zar* change *z* to *c* before the letter *e*.

Rezar   to pray

Present Indicative: rezo, rezas, etc.   I pray, etc.

Imperfect: rezaba, etc.   I was praying, etc.

Preterit: *recé*, rezaste, rezó, etc.   I prayed, etc.

Future: rezaré, etc.   I will pray, etc.

Conditional: rezaría, etc.   I would pray, etc.

Present Participle: rezando   praying

Past Participle: rezado   prayed

Present Subjunctive: *rece, reces, rece, recemos, recéis, recen,*   I may pray, etc.

Imperfect Subjunctive: rezara (rezase), etc.   I might pray, etc.

Present Perfect Subjunctive: haya rezado, etc.   I may have prayed, etc.

Pluperfect Subjunctive: hubiera (hubiese) rezado, etc.   I might have prayed, etc.

Others:

abrazar to embrace	*rechazar* to reject
alcanzar to reach, achieve	*sollozar* to sob
amenazar to threaten	*empezar** to begin
analizar to analyze	*almorzar** to eat lunch
cruzar to cross	*tropezar** to stumble
lanzar to throw	* see page 85

Verbs ending in *-guar* change *gu* to *gü* before *e*. The *u* requires a diaeresis (¨)before *e* to preserve the *u* sound.

Averiguar   to find out, verify

Present Indicative: averiguo, etc.   I find out, etc.

Imperfect: averiguaba, etc.   I was finding out, etc.

Preterit: *averigüé*, averiguaste, averiguó, etc.   I found out, etc.

Future: averiguaré, etc.   I will find out, etc.

Conditional: averiguaría, etc.   I would find out, etc.

Present Participle: averiguando   finding out

Past Participle: averiguado   found out

Present Subjunctive: *averigüe, averigües, averigüe, averigüemos, averigüéis, averigüen*   I may find out, etc.

Imperfect Subjunctive: averiguara (averiguase), etc.   I might find out, etc.

Present Perfect Subjunctive: haya averiguado, etc.   I may have found out, etc.

Pluperfect Subjunctive: hubiera (hubiese) averiguado, etc.   I might have found out, etc.

Others:

apaciguar   to pacify

menguar   to decrease

santiguar   to bless

Para practicar

Write in the *present subjunctive* in the person indicated:

tú:

secar	colocar	obligar	entregar	amenazar	analizar
_____	_____	_____	_____	_____	_____

averiguar	menguar
_____	_____

ellos

alcanzar	abrazar	llegar	castigar	arriesgar	rascar
_____	_____	_____	_____	_____	_____

replicar	explicar
_____	_____

Write in the *first-person singular preterit indicative*:

yo

explicar	sacar	indicar	negar	llegar	castigar
_____	_____	_____	_____	_____	_____

rogar	replicar	empezar	cruzar	rechazar	almorzar
_____	_____	_____	_____	_____	_____

marcar	apaciguar	santiguar
_____	_____	_____

Mastery Test

A. Translate into English:

1. él explique _____

2. Ud. marcara _____

3. yo apague _____

4. abracé _____

5. entregué _____

6. tropecemos _____

7. ellos sequen _____

8. castigues _____

9. Ud. rechace _____

10. averigües _____

11. tú repliques _____

12. carguemos _____

13. amenaces _____

14. mengüé _____

15. saqué _____

B. Translate into Spanish:

1. we may pacify _____

2. I paid _____

3. they may take out _____

4. I did not find out _____

5. you (s., fam.) may punish _____

_____

6. he may not place _____

7. I risked _____

8. we may tire _____

9. she may not reply _____

10. you (s., fam.) may cross _____

_____

11. you (pl., fam.) may beg _____

_____

12. I indicated _____

A. Translate into English: (*continued*)

16. santigüemos _____

17. él llegue _____

18. Uds. analicen _____

19. apacigüen _____

20. él alcance _____

B. Translate into Spanish: (*continued*)

13. he prays _____

14. you (s., fam.) may throw _____

_____

15. they may arrive _____

16. I did not explain _____

17. we may not analyze _____

18. you (pl., fam.) may reply _____

_____

19. I threw _____

20. I sobbed _____

Some verbs ending in -cer and -cir preceded by a consonant change c to z before o or a.

Vencer to conquer

Present Indicative: *venzo*, vences, etc.   I conquer, etc.

Imperfect: vencía, etc.   I was conquering, etc.

Preterit: vencí, etc.   I conquered, etc.

Future: venceré, etc.   I will conquer, etc.

Conditional: vencería, etc.   I would conquer, etc.

Present Participle: venciendo   conquering

Past Participle: vencido   conquered

Present Subjunctive: *venza, venzas, venza, venzamos, venzáis, venzan*   I may conquer, etc.

Imperfect Subjunctive: venciera, (venciese), etc.   I might conquer, etc.

Present Perfect Subjunctive: haya vencido, etc.   I may have conquered, etc.

Pluperfect Subjunctive: hubiera (hubiese) vencido, etc.   I might have conquered, etc.

Others:

convencer   to convince

ejercer   to exercise

esparcir   to scatter

Verbs ending in *-ger* or *-gir* change *g* to *j* before an *o* or *a*.

Escoger   to choose

Present Indicative: *escojo*, escoges, etc.   I choose, etc.

Imperfect: escogía, etc.   I was choosing, etc.

Preterit: escogí, etc.   I chose, etc.

Future: escogeré, etc.   I will choose, etc.

Conditional: escogería, etc.   I would choose, etc.

Present Participle: escogiendo   choosing

Past Participle: escogido   chosen

Present Subjunctive: *escoja, escojas, escoja, escojamos, escojáis, escojan*   I may choose, etc.

Imperfect Subjunctive: escogiera (escogiese), etc.   I might choose, etc.

Present Perfect Subjunctive: haya escogido, etc.   I may have chosen, etc.

Pluperfect Subjunctive: hubiera (hubiese) escogido, etc.   I might have chosen, etc.

Others:

dirigir to direct	*acoger* to welcome
coger to catch, seize, take	*encoger* to shrink
fingir to pretend	*corregir* to correct*
exigir to demand	*elegir* to elect, choose*
infligir to inflict	* see page 86

Verbs ending in *-guir* drop the *u* before *o* or *a*.

Distinguir   to distinguish

Present Indicative: *distingo*, distingues, etc.   I distinguish, etc.

Imperfect: distinguía, etc.   I was distinguishing, etc.

Preterit: distinguí, etc.   I distinguished, etc.

Future: distinguiré, etc.   I will distinguish, etc.

Conditional: distinguiría, etc.   I would distinguish, etc.

Present Participle: distinguiendo   distinguishing

Past Participle: distinguido   distinguished

Present Subjunctive: *distinga, distingas, distinga, distingamos, distingáis, distingan*   I may distinguish, etc.

Imperfect Subjunctive: distinguiera (distinguiese) etc.   I might distinguish, etc.

Present Perfect Subjunctive: haya distinguido, etc.   I may have distinguished, etc.

Pluperfect Subjunctive: hubiera (hubiese) distinguido, etc.   I might have distinguished, etc.

Others:

extinguir to extinguish	*perseguir* to persecute, pursue;*
seguir to follow;*	*proseguir* to prosecute, pursue*
conseguir to get, obtain;*	* see page 86

Verbs ending in *-quir* change *qu* to *c* before *o* or *a*.

Delinquir   to break the law

Present Indicative: *delinco*, delinques, etc.   I break the law, etc.
Imperfect: delinquía, etc.   I was breaking the law, etc.
Preterit: delinquí, etc.   I broke the law, etc.
Future: delinquiré, etc.   I will break the law, etc.
Conditional: delinquiría, etc.   I would break the law, etc.
Present Participle: delinquiendo   breaking the law
Past Participle: delinquido   broken the law
Present Subjunctive: *delinca, delincas, delinca, delincamos, delincáis, delincan*   I may break the law, etc.
Imperfect Subjunctive:delinquiera (delinquiese), etc.   I might break the law, etc.
Present Perfect Subjunctive: haya delinquido, etc.   I may have broken the law, etc.
Pluperfect Subjunctive: hubiera (hubiese) delinquido, etc.   I might have broken the law, etc.

Para practicar

Write the infinitives in the tense and person indicated:

Present indicative   **yo**

encoger	dirigir	coger	exigir	ejercer	convencer
_____	_____	_____	_____	_____	_____

esparcir	extinguir	delinquir	acoger
_____	_____	_____	_____

Present subjunctive   **nosotros**

extinguir	delinquir	distinguir	escoger	infligir	fingir
_____	_____	_____	_____	_____	_____

coger	esparcir	ejercer	dirigir
_____	_____	_____	_____

Aplicación

Translate into English:

1. ejerzo _____
2. Ud. convenció _____
3. esparciré _____
4. acogías _____
5. ellos distingan _____
6. finjamos _____
7. Uds. han convencido _____
8. dirigiré _____
9. él seguiría _____
10. extingas _____
11. ejercías _____
12. exijo _____
13. seguí _____
14. extinguiste _____
15. ellos convenzan _____
16. fingí _____
17. él delinquió _____
18. ellos cojan _____
19. extingo _____
20. delincáis _____

Mastery Test

Translate into Spanish:

1. you (s., fam.) might conquer _____
2. I may inflict _____
3. I distinguish _____
4. we exercised _____
5. I do not demand _____
6. you (s., fam.) may not distinguish _____
7. he will not convince _____
8. will you (pl., for.) choose? _____
9. let us not extinguish _____
10. I scattered _____

11. we directed _____

12. he distinguished _____

13. I break the law _____

14. you (s., fam.) exercise _____

15. he may welcome _____

16. they may extinguish _____

17. they may not convince _____

18. I pretend _____

19. you (pl., fam.) will distinguish _____

20. you (s., fam.) may not break the law _____

Verbs ending in -eer change the i to y in the third-person singular and plural of the preterit, all persons of the imperfect subjunctive and the present participle.

Creer   to believe

Present Indicative: creo, etc.   I believe, etc.

Imperfect: creía, etc.   I was believing, etc.

Preterit: creí, creíste, *creyó*, creímos, creísteis, *creyeron*   I believed, etc.

Future: creeré, etc.   I will believe, etc.

Conditional: creería, etc.   I would believe, etc.

Present Participle: *creyendo*   believing

Past Participle: creído   believed

Present Subjunctive: crea, etc.   I may believe, etc.

Imperfect Subjunctive: *creyera* (*creyese*), etc.   I might believe, etc.

Present Perfect Subjunctive: haya creído, etc.   I may have believed, etc.

Pluperfect Subjunctive: hubiera (hubiese) creído, etc.   I might have believed, etc.

Additional Note: -er and -ir verbs whose stems end in a vowel have a written accent on the i of the past participle. The past participle of such verbs is otherwise regular. Example: *creer   creído*.

Others:

leer	reír*
poseer	oír*
traer*	huir*
caer*	

* See individual conjugations for these verbs (*traer*, p. 116; *caer*, p. 97; *reír*, pp. 86–87; *oír*, p. 108; *huir*, p. 87).

Most verbs ending in *-cer* or *-cir* preceded by a vowel add *z* before *c* when followed by *o* or *a*.

Conocer to know, be acquainted with

Present Indicative: *conozco*, conoces, etc.   I know, etc.

Imperfect: conocía, etc.   I was knowing, etc.

Preterit: conocí, etc.   I knew, etc.

Future: conoceré, etc.   I will know, etc.

Conditional: conocería, etc.   I would know, etc.

Present Participle: conociendo   knowing

Past Participle: conocido   known

Present Subjunctive: *conozca, conozcas, conozca, conozcamos, conozcáis, conozcan*   I may know, etc.

Imperfect Subjunctive: conociera (conociese), etc.   I might know, etc.

Present Perfect Subjunctive: haya conocido, etc.   I may have known, etc.

Pluperfect Subjunctive: hubiera (hubiese) conocido, etc.   I might have known, etc.

Others:

agradecer to thank	*desaparecer* to disappear
reconocer to recognize	*enriquecerse* to become rich
desconocer to be unacquainted	*aparecer* to appear
complacer to please	*parecer* to seem
aborrecer to hate	*merecer* to deserve
compadecer to pity	*obedecer* to obey
carecer to lack	*ofrecer* to offer

Some verbs ending in *-iar* accent the *i* of the stem in all forms of the present indicative and present subjunctive, except the *nosotros* and *vosotros* forms.

Enviar to send

Present Indicative: *envío, envías*, envía, enviamos, enviáis, *envían*   I send, etc.

Imperfect: enviaba, etc.   I was sending, etc.

Preterit: envié, etc.   I sent, etc.

Future: enviaré, etc.   I will send, etc.

Conditional: enviaría, etc.   I would send, etc.

Present Participle: enviando   sending

Past Participle: enviado   sent

Present Subjunctive: *envíe, envíes, envíe*, enviemos, enviéis, *envíen*   I may sent, etc.

Imperfect Subjunctive: enviara (enviase), etc.   I might send, etc.

Present Perfect Subjunctive: haya enviado, etc.   I may have sent, etc.

Pluperfect Subjunctive: hubiera (hubiese) enviado, etc.   I might have sent, etc.

Others:

desafiar to defy, challenge
confiar to trust
desconfiar to mistrust
guiar to guide

Verbs ending in *-uar* preceded by any consonant except *c* or *g* accent the *u* in all forms of the present indicative and present subjunctive except the *nosotros* and *vosotros* forms.

Continuar   to continue

Present Indicative: *continúo, continúas, continúa*, continuamos, continuáis, *continúan*   I continue, etc.

Imperfect: continuaba, etc.   I was continuing, etc.

Preterit: continué, etc.   I continued, etc.

Future: continuaré etc.   I will continue, etc.

Conditional: continuaría, etc.   I would continue, etc.

Present Participle: continuando   continuing

Past Participle: continuado   continued

Present Subjunctive: *continúe, continúes, continúe*, continuemos, continuéis, *continúen*   I may continue, etc.

Imperfect Subjunctive: continuara (continuase), etc.   I might continue, etc.

Present Perfect Subjunctive: haya continuado, etc.   I may have continued, etc.

Pluperfect Subjunctive: hubiera (hubiese) continuado, etc.   I might have continued, etc.

Others:
insinuar   to insinuate
habituarse   to grow accustomed to
descontinuar   to discontinue
graduarse   to graduate, be graduated

Para practicar

Write the infinitives in the tense and person indicated:

Present subjunctive **tú**

aparecer	ofrecer	merecer	reconocer	compadecer	confiar
_____	_____	_____	_____	_____	_____

guiar	descontinuar
_____	_____

Present indicative **yo**

desafiar	parecer	obedecer	agradecer	insinuar	desconfiar
_____	_____	_____	_____	_____	_____

Preterit **Uds.**

leer	poseer	enviar	continuar	conocer	ofrecer
_____	_____	_____	_____	_____	_____

Aplicación

Change each verb to the corresponding tense in the plural:

1. estoy leyendo _____

2. envías _____

3. continúes _____

4. ofrezco _____

5. Ud. desafíe _____

6. aborrezcas _____

7. yo merezca _____

8. Ud. aparezca _____

9. guío _____

10. desconoció _____

11. poseyó _____

12. Ud. insinúe _____

13. se enriquezca _____

14. parecí _____

15. me habitué _____

16. yo creyese _____

17. Ud. complacía _____

18. ella desconfía _____

19. descontinúo _____

20. reconozco _____

Mastery Test

Translate into Spanish:

1. did she read? _____

2. we may disappear _____

3. he may continue _____

4. they may send _____

5. I was possessing _____

6. you (s., for.) may not know _____

7. we may mistrust _____

8. I do not guide _____

9. you (s., fam.) might read _____

_____

10. he may pity _____

_____

11. I was sending _____

12. you (s., fam.) may discontinue _____

_____

13. we were believing _____

14. you (pl., fam.) disappear _____

_____

15. they sent _____

16. she did not believe _____

17. I hated _____

18. do you (s., fam.) trust? _____

_____

19. they may know _____

20. she continued _____

Orthographic Stem Changes

Verbs ending in *-gar* with stem-vowel *e* or *o* change *g* to *gu* before *e* and also change the stem vowel from *e* to *ie* and *o* to *ue* in all forms of the present indicative and present subjunctive, except the *nosotros* and *vosotros* forms (see pages 62 and 72).

Negar   to deny

Present Indicative: niego, niegas, niega, negamos, negáis, *niegan*   I deny, etc.

Preterit: negué, negaste, etc.   I denied, etc.

Present Subjunctive: niegue, niegues, niegue, neguemos, neguéis, nieguen   I may deny, etc.

All other forms are regular.

Others:
cegar   to blind
desnegar   to contradict
rogar   to ask, beg

Colgar   to hang up

cuelgo, cuelgas, cuelga, colgamos, colgáis, *cuelgan*   I hang up, etc.

colgué, colgaste, etc.   I hung up, etc.

cuelgue, cuelgues, cuelgue, colguemos, colguéis, cuelguen   I may hang up, etc.

Note one verb that ends in *-gar* and has the stem vowel *u* change to *ue*, in addition to the orthographic change of *g* to *gu*.

Jugar   to play

Present Indicative: juego, juegas, juega, jugamos, jugáis, *juegan*   I play, etc.

Preterit: jugué, jugaste, etc.   I played, etc.

Present Subjunctive: juegue, juegues, juegue, juguemos, juguéis, jueguen   I may play, etc.

All other forms are regular. *Jugar* is the only verb of this type.

Verbs ending in *-zar* with the stem vowel *e* or *o* change *z* to *c* before *e* and stem vowels *e* to *ie* and *o* to *ue* in all forms of the present indicative and present subjunctive except the *nosotros* and *vosotros* forms (see pages 62 and 73).

Empezar   to begin

Present Indicative: empiezo, empiezas, empieza, empezamos, empezáis, *empiezan* I begin, etc.

Preterit: empecé, empezaste, etc.   I began, etc.

Present Subjunctive: empiece, empieces, empiece, empecemos, empecéis, *empiecen*   I may begin, etc.

Almorzar   to eat lunch

almuerzo, almuerzas, almuerza, almorzamos, almorzáis, *almuerzan*   I eat lunch, etc.

almorcé, almorzaste, etc.   I ate lunch, etc.

almuerce, almuerces, almuerce, almorcemos, almorcéis, almuercen   I may eat lunch, etc.

86

All other forms are regular.

Others:
tropezar   to stumble
esforzarse   to try hard

Verbs ending in *-egir* change *g* to *j* before *o* or *a* and stem-vowel *e* to *i* in accordance with rules for stem-changing verbs of Class III (see pages 69 and 77).

Colegir   to collect

Present Indicative: *colijo*, *coliges*, *colige*, colegimos, colegís, *coligen*   I collect, etc.
Preterit: colegí, colegiste, *coligió*, colegimos, colegisteis, *coligieron*   I collected, etc.
Present Participle: *coligiendo*   collecting
Present Subjunctive: *colija*, *colijas*, *colija*, *colijamos*, *colijáis*, *colijan*   I may collect, etc.
Imperfect Subjunctive: *coligiera* (*coligiese*), *coligieras*, *coligiera*, *coligieramos*, *coligierais*, *coligieran*   I might collect, etc.

Others:
corregir   to correct
elegir   to elect

Verbs in *-eguir* change *gu* to *g* before *o* or *a* and *e* to *i* in accordance with rules for stem-changing verbs of Class III.

Seguir   to follow

Present Indicative: *sigo*, *sigues*, *sigue*, seguimos, seguís, *siguen*   I follow, etc.
Preterit: seguí, seguiste, *siguió*, seguimos, seguisteis, *siguieron*   I followed, etc.
Present Participle: *siguiendo*   following
Present Subjunctive: *siga*, *sigas*, *siga*, *sigamos*, *sigáis*, *sigan*   I may follow, etc.
Imperfect Subjunctive: *siguiera* (*siguiese*) etc.   I might follow, etc.

Stem has *i* throughout imperfect subjunctive.

Others:
consequir   to get, obtain
perseguir   to persecute, pursue
proseguir   to prosecute, pursue

Verbs in *-eír* change *e* to *i* in accordance with rules of stem-changing verbs of Class III. In addition, when the stem is stressed, the *i* has a written accent. When the stem is not changed and is followed by a stressed *i* in the ending, the *i* requires a written accent, as does the infinitive.

Reir   to laugh

Present Indicative: *río*, *ríes*, *ríe*, reímos, reís, *ríen*   I laugh, etc.
Preterit: reí, reíste, *rió*, reímos, reísteis, *rieron*   I laughed, etc.
Present Participle: *riendo*   laughing

Past Participle: reído
Present Subjunctive: *ría, rías, ría, riamos, riáis, rían*   I may laugh, etc.
Imperfect Subjunctive: *riera* (*riese*) etc.   I might laugh, etc.

Others:
sonreír   to smile

Verbs ending in *-uir* insert *y* before all endings after an accented stem and change unaccented *i* to *y* before *e* or *a* in endings (see page 80).

Huir   to flee

Present Indicative: *huyo, huyes, huye,* huímos, huís, *huyen*   I flee, etc.
Preterit: huí, huiste, *huyó,* huimos, huisteis, *huyeron*   I fled, etc.
Present Participle: *huyendo*   fleeing
Present Subjunctive: *huya, huyas, huya, huyamos, huyáis, huyan*   I may flee, etc.
Imperfect Subjunctive: *huyera* (*huyese*), etc.   I might flee, etc.

Others:
concluir   to conclude   *incluir*   to include
destruir   to destroy   *restituir*   to restore
instruir   to instruct   *constituir*   to constitute, consist
construir   to construct

Para practicar

Write the infinitives in the tense and person indicated:

Present indicative **yo**
corregir   rogar   cegar   tropezar   conseguir   contruir

_____   _____   _____   _____   _____   _____

sonreír

_____

Present indicative Ud.

desnegar	perseguir	reír	destruir	esforzarse	elegir
————————	————————	————————	————————	————————	————————

jugar

————————

Preterit yo

colegir	rogar	almorzar	incluir	reír	proseguir
————————	————————	————————	————————	————————	————————

cegar

————————

Preterit ellos

corregir	consequir	sonreír	restituir	elegir	instruir
————————	————————	————————	————————	————————	————————

negar

————————

Present subjunctive tú

cegar	jugar	tropezar	corregir	proseguir	destruir
————————	————————	————————	————————	————————	————————

reír

————————

Present subjunctive nosotros

desnegar	esforzarse	elegir	consequir	sonreír	concluir
————————	————————	————————	————————	————————	————————

jugar

————————

Imperfect subjunctive **él**

corregir	proseguir	reír	construir	elegir	constituir
_____	_____	_____	_____	_____	_____

conseguir

_____

Present participle

colegir	colgar	almorzar	sonreír	destruir	perseguir
_____	_____	_____	_____	_____	_____

incluir

_____

Past participle

cegar	empezar	elegir	seguir	reír	concluir
_____	_____	_____	_____	_____	_____

huir

_____

Aplicación

Change from singular to plural in the same tense:

1. ruegue Ud. _____

2. tropiezo _____

3. él almuerce _____

4. cegué _____

5. escojo _____

6. empecé _____

7. juega _____

8. me esforcé _____

9. cuelgues _____

10. empiezo _____

11. huye _____

12. Ud. sonrió _____

13. él destruyó _____

14. yo concluyese _____

15. has huido _____

16. él corrija _____

17. Ud. consiguió _____

18. sigo _____

19. yo escogiera _____

20. consigas _____

21. él estaba siguiendo _____

22. yo elija _____

23. corrijo _____

24. persigue _____

25. incluyas _____

26. yo concluía _____

27. Ud. había reído _____

28. instruyo _____

29. Ud. ha restituido _____

30. está sonriendo _____

Mastery Test
Orthographic changes and orthographic-stem changes:

A. Write in English:

1. yo apague _____

2. ejerzo _____

3. envías _____

4. tropiezo _____

5. ¡extinga Ud.! _____

6. ofrezco _____

7. entregué _____

8. ellos distingan _____

9. desconozcas _____

10. jugué _____

11. finjamos _____

12. guío _____

13. Ud. almuerce _____

14. corrijo _____

15. él poseyó _____

B. Write in Spanish:

1. I paid _____

2. I might choose _____

3. did she read? _____

4. I did not find out _____

5. they followed _____

6. he may continue _____

7. he may not place _____

8. you (s., fam.) may not extinguish _____
_____

9. they may send _____

10. we may arrive _____

11. did you (s., for.) obtain? _____
_____

12. you (s., fam.) may not know _____
_____

16. repliques _____

17. ellos cojan _____

18. Ud. insinúe _____

19. amenaces _____

20. exijo _____

21. yo creyese _____

22. marqué _____

23. consigas _____

24. sonrío _____

25. Ud. ruegue _____

26. ellos convenzan _____

27. Ud. concluyese _____

28. Uds. apacigüen _____

29. delincáis _____

30. destruyó _____

13. you (s., for.) may cross _____

_____

14. I follow _____

15. I don't guide _____

16. I begged _____

17. I break the law _____

18. you (s., fam.) might read _____

_____

19. you (pl., fam.) may begin _____

_____

20. he may direct _____

21. they destroyed _____

22. I did not explain _____

23. I pretend _____

24. you (s., fam.) do not laugh _____

_____

25. you (s., for.) may reply _____

_____

26. they may not convince _____

_____

27. we were believing _____

28. I threw _____

29. you (s., fam.) may choose _____

_____

30. we might conclude _____

Repaso general 1

A. Change each verb from singular to plural in the same tense:

1. parto _____

2. comprendiste _____

3. él vivía _____

4. asistiré _____

5. tomarías _____

6. estoy escribiendo _____

7. estaba vistiéndose _____

8. he hablado _____

9. Ud. había vendido _____

10. habrás asistido _____

11. él habría bebido _____

12. conteste Ud. _____

13. aprendieras _____

14. él haya entrado _____

15. yo hubiera tomado _____

16. acuerdo _____

17. se acueste _____

18. yo consienta _____

19. no se divierte _____

20. Ud. pidió _____

21. leyó _____

22. río _____

23. negué _____

B. Write in Spanish:

1. they fear _____

2. you (s., fam.) used to drink _____

_____

3. you (pl., fam.) may show _____

_____

4. I began _____

5. did you (s., fam.) speak? _____

_____

6. they served _____

7. we were believing _____

8. you (pl., fam.) might read _____

_____

9. he would not write _____

10. he notices _____

11. they may not convince _____

_____

12. he may not begin _____

13. you (s., fam.) were speaking _____

_____

14. it is snowing _____

15. you (pl., for.) may explain _____

_____

16. you (pl., fam.) may direct _____

24. Ud. incluya _____

_____

25. juegues _____

17. I will have taught _____

26. reconozco _____

18. they might ask for _____

27. Ud. persiguió _____

19. you (s., fam.) do not laugh _____

_____

28. almuerces _____

29. averigüe _____

20. I do not guide _____

30. distingo _____

21. let us fear _____

22. I choose _____

23. do you (s., fam.) continue? _____

_____

24. I did not explain _____

25. he was selling _____

26. I begged _____

27. they destroyed _____

28. you (s., fam.) may choose _____

_____

29. they used to carry _____

30. he sends _____

Repaso general 2

A. Make each simple tense into a compound one in the same person:

1. temía _____

2. parto _____

3. vivían _____

4. necesitaré _____

B. Write in Spanish:

1. they would have left _____

2. they may read _____

3. we might conclude _____

4. she is not studying _____

94

A. Make each simple tense into a compound one in the same person: (*continued*)

5. partiríamos _____

6. comas _____

7. vendiésemos _____

8. Ud. rió _____

9. restituyes _____

10. envían _____

11. descontinúo _____

12. obedezco _____

13. creyó _____

14. desaparezcan _____

15. yo poseyera _____

16. tropieza _____

17. distinga Ud. _____

18. juegan _____

19. expliquen _____

20. consigo _____

21. hirió _____

22. eliges _____

23. él delinca _____

24. sonríen _____

25. destruyeron _____

26. hablaréis _____

27. aprendí _____

B. Write in Spanish: (*continued*)

5. they understand _____

6. I paid _____

7. you (s., fam.) may cross _____

_____

8. you (s., for.) would carry _____

_____

9. we may close _____

10. I might choose _____

11. did you (s., fam.) obtain? _____

_____

12. we might not attend _____

13. you (pl., fam.) might prevent _____

_____

14. did she read? _____

15. let us arrive _____

16. do you (s., for.) open? _____

_____

17. they prevented _____

18. I did not find out _____

19. you (pl., fam.) do not cross _____

_____

20. you (s., fam.) will enter _____

_____

28. durmió _____

29. corrigiéramos _____

30. huyera _____

21. I dress myself _____

22. they followed _____

23. I close _____

24. would you (pl., for.) read? _____

_____

25. they may die _____

26. continue! (pl., for.) _____

27. I follow _____

28. you (pl., for.) will have lived _____

_____

29. you (pl., fam.) may lose _____

_____

30. he may not look for _____

Irregular Verbs

Andar   to walk

Present Indicative: ando, andas, etc.   I walk, etc.

Imperfect: andaba, etc.   I was walking, etc.

Preterit: *anduve, anduviste, anduvo, anduvimos, anduvisteis, anduvieron*   I walked, etc.

Future: andaré, etc.   I will walk, etc.

Conditional: andaría, etc.   I would walk, etc.

Present Participle: andando   walking

Past Participle: andado   walked

Present Subjunctive: ande, etc.   I may walk, etc.

Imperfect Subjunctive: anduviera (*anduviese*) *anduvieras, anduviera, anduviéramos, anduvierais, anduvieran*   I might walk, etc.

Present Perfect Subjunctive: haya andado, etc.   I may have walked, etc.

Pluperfect Subjunctive: hubiera (hubiese) andado, etc.   I might have walked, etc

Asir   to seize

Present Indicative: *asgo*, ases, etc.   I seize, etc.

Imperfect: asía, etc.   I was seizing, etc.

Preterit: *así, asiste*, etc.   I seized, etc.

Future: asiré, etc.   I will seize, etc.

Conditonal: asiría, etc.   I would seize, etc.

Present Participle: asiendo   seizing

Past Participle: asido   seized

Present Subjunctive: *asga, asgas, asga, asgamos, asgáis, asgan*   I may seize, etc.

Imperfect Subjunctive: asiera (asiese), etc.   I might seize, etc.

Present Perfect Subjunctive: haya asido, etc.   I may have seized, etc.

Pluperfect Subjunctive: hubiera (hubiese) asido, etc.   I might have seized, etc.

Other:
desasir   to loosen

Caber   to be room for, to fit

Present Indicative: *quepo*, cabes, etc.   I fit, etc.

Imperfect: cabía, etc.   I was fitting, etc.

Preterit: *cupe, cupiste, cupo, cupimos, cupisteis, cupieron*   I fitted, etc.

Future: *cabré, cabrás, cabrá, cabremos, cabréis, cabrán*   I will fit, etc.

Conditional: *cabría*, etc.   I would fit, etc.

Present Participle: cabiendo   fitting

Past Participle: cabido   fitted

Present Subjunctive: quepa, quepas, quepa, quepamos, quepáis, quepan   I may fit, etc.
Imperfect Subjunctive: cupiera (*cupiese*), etc.   I might fit, etc.
Present Perfect Subjunctive: haya cabido, etc.   I may have fitted, etc.
Pluperfect Subjunctive: hubiera (hubiese) cabido, etc.   I might have fitted, etc.

Caer   to fall

Present Indicative: caigo, caes, cae, caemos, caéis, caen   I fall, etc.
Imperfect: caía, etc.   I was falling, etc.
Preterit: caí, caíste, *cayó*, caímos, caísteis, *cayeron*   I fell, etc.
Future: caeré, etc.   I will fall, etc.
Conditional: caería, etc.   I would fall, etc.
Present Participle: cayendo   falling
Past Participle: caído   fallen
Present Subjunctive: caiga, caigas, caiga, caigamos, caigáis, caigan   I may fall, etc.
Imperfect Subjunctive: cayera, (*cayese*), etc.   I might fall, etc.
Present Perfect Subjunctive: haya caído, etc.   I may have fallen, etc.
Pluperfect Subjunctive: hubiera (hubiese) caído, etc.   I might have fallen, etc.

Others:
decaer   to decline, decay, fade

Para practicar

Write the infinitives in the tense and person indicated:

Present indicative **yo**

desasir	caber	andar	decaer
_____	_____	_____	_____

Uds.

asir	andar	caer	caber
_____	_____	_____	_____

Preterit **él**

desasir	caber	andar	caer
_____	_____	_____	_____

Future **nosotros**

asir	decaer	caber	andar
_____	_____	_____	_____

Present subjunctive **tú**

desasir   caer   caber   andar

_____   _____   _____   _____

Imperfect subjunctive **vosotros**

decaer   andar   caber   asir

_____   _____   _____   _____

Aplicación

Translate into English:

1. ellos caerían _____

2. cabremos _____

3. hayas caído _____

4. andabais _____

5. Uds. cabrían _____

6. ellos cayeron _____

7. decaeríais _____

8. cupiste _____

9. desasimos _____

10. anduvimos _____

11. decaigamos _____

12. ellos quepan _____

13. Uds. caigan _____

14. asiré _____

15. decaímos _____

16. él caerá _____

17. yo cupiera _____

18. caigo _____

19. quepo _____

20. ellos asgan _____

21. decayeras _____

22. andaremos _____

23. ellos hubieran asido _____

24. ellos habrían andado _____

25. Uds. desasirán _____

26. ellos están decayendo _____

27. andemos _____

28. él habrá decaído _____

29. ellos anduviesen _____

30. Uds. asen _____

Mastery Test

Write in Spanish:

1. they would not fall _____

2. I might have walked _____

3. they would seize _____

4. were you (s., fam.) walking? _____

_____

5. they are fading _____

6. they might loosen _____

7. you (pl., fam.) would decline _____

_____

8. will I walk? _____

9. I loosen _____

10. he walked _____

11. did he fit? _____

12. we were loosening _____

13. they declined _____

14. we should have fitted _____

_____

15. I shall not fall _____

16. he fits _____

17. we might walk _____

18. he had seized _____

19. he would not have fallen _____

_____

20. he may walk _____

21. you (s., fam.) had seized _____

_____

22. I walk _____

23. you (pl., for.) would fall _____

_____

24. did he seize? _____

25. he has fallen _____

26. we may fit _____

27. you (s., fam.) used to walk _____

_____

28. we were falling _____

29. you (s., fam.) may have walked _____

_____

30. we had fitted _____

31. I may have seized _____

32. you (pl., fam.) fell _____

33. I might have fallen _____

34. you (s., for.) fitted _____

35. I might fit _____   38. we might fall _____

36. you (s., fam.) decline _____   39. I may not fit _____

37. they may seize _____   40. you (pl., fam.) may fall _____

_____

Conducir   to lead, conduct

Present Indicative: *conduzco*, conduces, etc.   I lead, etc.

Imperfect: conducía, etc.   I was leading, etc.

Preterit: *conduje, condujiste, condujo, condujimos, condujisteis, condujeron*   I led, etc.

Future: conduciré, etc.   I will lead, etc.

Conditional: conduciría, etc.   I would lead, etc.

Present Participle: conduciendo   leading

Past Participle: conducido   led

Present Subjunctive: *conduzca, conduzcas, conduzca, conduzcamos, conduzcáis, conduzcan*   I may lead, etc.

Imperfect Subjunctive: *condujera* (*condujese*), etc.   I might lead, etc.

Present Perfect Subjunctive: haya conducido, etc.   I may have led, etc.

Pluperfect Subjunctive: hubiera (hubiese) conducido, etc.   I might have led, etc.

Others:
deducir   to deduce
traducir   to translate
producir   to produce

Dar   to give

Present Indicative: *doy*, das, da, damos, *dais*, dan   I give, etc.

Imperfect: daba, etc.   I was giving, etc.

Preterit: *di, diste, dio, dimos, disteis, dieron*   I gave, etc.

Future   daré, etc.   I will gave, etc.

Conditional: daría, etc.   I would give, etc.

Present Participle: dando   giving

Past Participle: dado   given

Present Sujunctive: *dé, des, dé, demos, deis, den*   I may give, etc.

Imperfect Subjunctive: *diera*, (*diese*), etc.   I might give, etc.

Present Perfect Subjunctive: haya dado, etc.   I may have given, etc.

Pluperfect Subjunctive: hubiera (hubiese) dado, etc.   I might have given, etc.

Decir   to say, tell

Present Indicative: *digo, dices, dice,* decimos, decís, *dicen*   to say, etc.

Imperfect: decía, etc.   I was saying, etc.

Preterit: *dije, dijiste, dijo, dijimos, dijisteis, dijeron*   I said, etc.

Future: *diré, dirás, dirá, diremos, diréis, dirán*   I will tell, etc.

Conditional: *dirás,* etc.   I would tell, etc.

Present Participle: *diciendo*   saying

Past Participle: *dicho*   said

Present Subjunctive: *diga, digas, diga, digamos, digáis, digan*   I may tell, etc.

Imperfect Subjunctive: *dijera* (*dijese*), etc.   I might say, etc.

Present Perfect Subjunctive: haya *dicho,* etc.   I may have said, etc.

Pluperfect Subjunctive: hubiera (hubiese) *dicho,* etc.   I might have said, etc.

Others:
maldecir   to curse
bendecir   to bless*

* Note that *maldecir* and *bendecir* are regular in the future and the conditional (*maldeciré, bendeciría,* etc.). The past participles of these verbs are also regular (*maldecido, bendecido*).

Errar   to err, to wander

Pesent Indicative: *yerro, yerras, yerra,* erramos, erráis, *yerran*   I wander, etc.

Imperfect: erraba, etc.   I was wandering, etc.

Preterit: erré, etc.   I wandered, etc.

Future: erraré, etc.   I will wander, etc.

Conditional: erraría, etc.   I would wander, etc.

Present participle: errando   wandering

Past Participle: errado   wandered

Present Subjunctive: *yerre, yerres, yerre,* erremos, erréis, *yerren*   I may wander, etc.

Imperfect Subjunctive: errara (errase), etc.   I might wander, etc.

Present Perfect Subjunctive: haya errado, etc.   I may have wandered, etc.

Pluperfect Subjunctive: hubiera (hubiese) errado, etc.   I might have wandered, etc.

Para practicar

Write the infinitives in the person and tense indicated:

Present indicative **yo**

deducir	maldecir	errar	dar	traducir
_____	_____	_____	_____	_____

Preterit **ellos**

producir	bendecir	dar	conducir	errar
_____	_____	_____	_____	_____

Future **Ud.**

traducir	maldecir	deducir	bendecir	dar
_____	_____	_____	_____	_____

Pluperfect indicative **Uds.**

dar	deducir	bendecir	errar	decir
_____	_____	_____	_____	_____

Present subjunctive **tú**

dar	producir	bendecir	errar	decir
_____	_____	_____	_____	_____

Imperfect subjunctive **nosotros**

errar	traducir	maldecir	dar	conducir
_____	_____	_____	_____	_____

Aplicación

Write in English:

1. dedujisteis _____

2. das _____

3. él dirá _____

4. erremos _____

5. conducíamos _____

6. ellos den _____

7. digamos _____

8. maldecías _____

9. él traduce _____

10. Ud. habría dado _____

11. ellos dijeron _____

12. yo haya dicho _____

13. ella condujo _____

14. doy _____

15. yerres _____

16. diríamos _____

17. yo deduzca _____

18. Ud. dio _____

19. ellos bendicen _____

20. Uds. yerran _____

21. él produciría _____

22. dieras _____

23. él dijera _____

24. yerro _____

25. ella tradujera _____

26. dábamos _____

27. ellos habrían maldicho _____

_____

28. erré _____

29. produzco _____

30. daré _____

Mastery Test

Write in Spanish:

1. you (s., fam.) will say _____

_____

2. you (pl., fam.) lead _____

3. let us wander _____

4. I may have told _____

5. he was not giving _____

6. you (s., fam.) translated _____

_____

7. he might bless _____

8. we will give _____

9. you (pl., for.) may produce _____

10. did he lead? _____

11. you (pl., fam.) might not say _____

_____

12. does he give? _____

13. I do wander _____

14. he might deduce _____

15. we would curse _____

16. they gave _____

17. I might produce _____

18. do not translate! (pl., for.) _____

19. are they saying? _____

20. they wandered _____

21. they might have given _____

_____

22. have you (pl., fam.) not told? _____

_____

23. I produce _____

24. he wanders _____

25. we will not tell _____

26. they were not saying _____

27. I do not give _____

28. I may deduce _____

29. they may not translate _____

_____

30. you (s., fam.) cursed _____

31. did you (pl., fam.) give? _____

_____

32. we will lead _____

33. you (s., for.) may give _____

_____

34. I bless _____

35. they produced _____

36. you (s., fam.) were translating _____

_____

37. he might not give _____

38. he may curse _____

39. they may have given _____

40. he may not lead _____

Estar   to be (in a state or condition)

Present Indicative: *estoy, estás, está,* estamos, estáis, *están*   I am, etc.

Imperfect: estaba, etc.   I was, etc.

Preterit: *estuve, estuviste, estuvo, estuvimos, estuvisteis, estuvieron*   I was, etc.

Future: estaré, etc.   I will be, etc.

Conditional: estaría, etc.   I would be, etc.

Present Participle: estando   being

Past Participle: estado   been

Present Subjunctive: *esté, estés, esté,* estemos, estéis, *estén*   I may be, etc.

Imperfect Subjunctive: estuviera (*estuviese*), etc.   I might be, etc.

Present Perfect Subjunctive: haya estado, etc.   I may have been, etc.

Pluperfect Subjunctive: hubiera (hubiese) estado, etc.   I might have been, etc.

Haber   to have (used only as an auxiliary with perfect tenses or in idiomatic expressions. Some tenses are defective, i.e., they do not have complete forms)

Present Indicative: *he, has, ha, hemos,* habéis, *han*   I have, etc.; *hay*   there is, are

Imperfect: había, etc.   I had, etc.; había   there was, were

Preterit: *hube,* hubiste, *hubo,* hubimos, hubisteis, hubieron   I had, etc.; *hubo*   there was, were

Future: *habré, habrás, habrá, habremos, habréis, habrán.*   I will have, etc.; *habrá*   there will be

Conditional: *habría,* etc.   I would have, etc.; *habría*   there would be

Present Participle: habiendo   having, there being

Past Participle: habido   ha (había, habrá, habría) habido   there has (had, will have, would have) been

Present Subjunctive: *haya, hayas, haya, hayamos, hayáis, hayan*   I may have, etc. *haya*   there may be

Imperfect Subjunctive: hubiera (*hubiese*), etc.   I might have, etc.; *hubiera* (*hubiese*) there might be
Present Perfect Subjunctive: haya habido   there may have been
Pluperfect Subjunctive: hubiera (hubiese) habido   there might have been

Hacer   to do, make

Present Indicative: *hago*, haces, hace, hacemos, hacéis, hacen   I do, etc.
Imperfect: hacía, etc.   I was doing, etc.
Preterit: *hice, hiciste, hizo, hicimos, hicisteis, hicieron*   I did, etc.
Future: *haré, harás, hará haremos, haréis, harán*   I will do, etc.
Conditional: *haría*, etc.   I would do, etc.
Present Participle: haciendo   doing
Past Participle: *hecho*   done
Present Subjunctive: *haga, hagas, haga, hagamos, hagáis, hagan*   I may do, etc.
Imperfect Subjunctive: hiciera (*hiciese*), etc.   I might do, etc.
Present Perfect Subjunctive: haya *hecho*, etc.   I may have done, etc.
Pluperfect Subjunctive: hubiera (hubiese) *hecho*, etc.   I might have done, etc.

Other:
satisfacer   to satisfy

Ir   to go

Present Indicative: *voy, vas, va, vamos, vais, van*   I go, etc.
Imperfect: *iba, ibas, iba, íbamos, ibais, iban*   I was going, etc.
Preterit: *fui, fuiste, fue, fuimos, fuisteis, fueron*   I went, etc.
Future: iré, etc.   I will go, etc.
Conditional: iría, etc.   I would go, etc.
Present Participle: *yendo*   going
Past Participle: ido   gone
Present Subjunctive: *vaya, vayas, vaya, vayamos, vayáis, vayan*   I may go, etc.
Imperfect Subjunctive: *fuera* (*fuese*), etc.   I might go, etc.
Present Perfect Subjunctive: haya ido, etc.   I may have gone, etc.
Pluperfect Subjunctive: hubiera (hubiese) ido, etc.   I might have gone, etc.

Para practicar

Change to the plural of the same tense:

1. voy _____

2. Ud. satisfaga _____

3. habrá _____

4. estoy _____

5. ibas _____

6. yo hubiera _____

7. he _____

8. estuvo _____

9. fui _____

10. hará _____

11. hubiste _____

12. hicieras _____

13. él vaya _____

14. estuvieras _____

15. has hecho _____

16. Ud. haya _____

17. fueras _____

18. satisfizo _____

19. Ud. esté _____

20. satisfago _____

Aplicación

Translate into English:

1. él habrá satisfecho _____

2. estamos _____

3. hay _____

4. fuiste _____

5. él haría _____

6. satisficiste _____

7. habría habido _____

8. hayas hecho _____

9. yo no estaría _____

10. satisfaré _____

11. ellos habían _____

12. hacíamos _____

13. ibais _____

14. satisficiésemos _____

15. haya habido _____

16. yo habría estado _____

17. Ud. satisfaga _____

18. estuvieras _____

19. habrías _____

20. hicimos _____

21. ellos estaban _____

22. él hiciera _____

23. él ha _____

24. no vayas _____

25. yo habría hecho _____

26. satisfacías _____

27. fuéramos _____

28. estén _____

29. estuve _____

30. va _____

Mastery Test

Write in Spanish:

1. we might have gone _____

2. I was (pret) _____

3. I may have done _____

4. they would have satisfied _____

_____

5. he was (imperfect) _____

6. they will not have gone _____

_____

7. we were not doing _____

8. you (pl., for.) will satisfy _____

_____

9. we are _____

10. I had done _____

11. he was going _____

12. I satisfied _____

13. we may be _____

14. there are not _____

15. we do not satisfy _____

16. does she go? _____

17. you (s., for.) will be _____

18. they did _____

19. we may satisfy _____

20. I might not be _____

21. there would have been _____

_____

22. you (s., fam.) might go _____

_____

23. he was satisfying _____

24. there will be _____

25. I may go _____

26. there might have been _____

_____

27. he may satisfy _____

28. you (s., fam.) will do _____

_____

29. there might be _____

30. they might have been _____

_____

31. you (pl., fam.) went _____

32. there has been _____

33. they may not do _____   37. there may be _____

34. I satisfy _____   38. we would do _____

35. they might have done _____   39. there was (imperfect) _____

36. I will not go _____   40. I am not _____

Oir   to hear

Present Indicative: *oigo, oyes, oye,* oímos, oís, *oyen*   I hear, etc.
Imperfect: oía, oías, etc.   I was hearing etc.
Preterit: oí, oíste, *oyó,* oímos, oísteis, *oyeron*   I heard, etc.
Future: oiré, etc.   I will hear, etc.
Conditional: oiría, etc.   I would hear, etc.
Present Participle: *oyendo*   hearing
Past Participle: oído   heard
Present Subjunctive: *oiga, oigas, oiga, oigamos, oigáis, oigan*   I may hear, etc.
Imperfect Subjunctive: *oyera (oyese),* etc.   I might hear, etc.
Present Perfect Subjunctive: haya oído, etc.   I may have heard, etc.
Pluperfect Subjunctive: hubiera (hubiese) oído, etc.   I might have heard, etc.

Oler   to smell

Present Indicative: *huelo, hueles, huele,* olemos, oléis, *huelen*   I smell, etc.
Imperfect: olía, etc.   I was smelling, etc.
Preterit: olí, oliste, etc.   I smelled, etc.
Future: oleré, etc.   I will smell, etc.
Conditional: olería, etc.   I would smell, etc.
Present Participle: oliendo   smelling
Past Participle: olido   smelled
Present Subjunctive: *huela, huelas, huela,* olamos, oláis, *huelan*   I may smell, etc.
Imperfect Subjunctive: oliera (oliese), etc.   I might smell, etc.
Present Perfect Subjunctive: haya olido, etc.   I may have smelled, etc.
Pluperfect Subjunctive: hubiera (hubiese) olido, etc.   I might have smelled, etc.

Poder   to be able

Present Indicative: *puedo puedes, puede,* podemos, podéis, *pueden,*   I can, am able, etc.
Imperfect: podía, etc.   I was able, could, etc.
Preterit: *pude, pudiste, pudo, pudimos, pudisteis, pudieron*   I was able, could etc.
Future: *podré, podrás, podra, podremos, podréis, podrán*   I will be able, etc.
Conditional: *podría,* etc.   I would be able, could etc.
Present Participle: *pudiendo*   being able

Past Participle: podido   been able

Present Subjunctive: *puede, puedas, pueda*, podamos, podáis, *puedan*   I may be able, etc.

Imperfect Subjunctive: *pudiera* (*pudiese*), etc.   I might be able, etc.

Present Perfect Subjunctive: haya podido, etc.   I may have been able, etc.

Pluperfect Subjunctive: hubiera (hubiese) podido, etc.   I might have been able, etc.

Poner   to put, place

Present Indicative: *pongo*, pones, pone, ponemos, ponéis, ponen   I put, etc.

Imperfect: ponía, etc.   I was putting, etc.

Preterit: *puse, pusiste, puso, pusimos, pusisteis, pusieron*   I put, did put, etc.

Future: *pondré, pondrás, pondrá, pondremos, pondréis, pondrán*   I will put, etc.

Conditional: *pondría*, etc.   I would put, etc.

Present Participle: poniendo   putting

Past Participle: *puesto*   put

Present Subjunctive: *ponga, pongas, ponga, pongamos, pongáis, pongan*   I may put, etc.

Imperfect Subjunctive: *pusiera* (*pusiese*), etc.   I might put, etc.

Present Perfect Subjunctive: haya *puesto*, etc.   I may have put, etc.

Pluperfect Subjunctive: hubiera (hubiese) *puesto*, etc.   I might have put, etc.

Others:

disponer to dispose	*imponer* to impose
exponer to expose	*proponer* to propose
componer to compose	*suponer* to suppose

Para practicar

Change the infinitives to the tense and person indicated:

Present indicative   **tú**

proponer	older	poder	oír	componer
_____	_____	_____	_____	_____

Preterit   **Uds.**

disponer	poder	oír	imponer	suponer
_____	_____	_____	_____	_____

Future   **yo**

disponer	exponer	imponer	proponer	suponer
_____	_____	_____	_____	_____

Present subjunctive **él**

componer	poder	oír	oler	exponer
_____	_____	_____	_____	_____

Present perfect subjunctive **nosotros**

oír	disponer	poner	suponer	poder
_____	_____	_____	_____	_____

Aplicación

Change the singular verb to plural, retaining the same tense:

1. él pusiera _____
2. yo pueda _____
3. él oiría _____
4. pudiste _____
5. dispones _____
6. yo oía _____
7. Ud. podrá _____
8. olió _____
9. he compuesto _____
10. habré podido _____
11. oiré _____
12. olerías _____
13. él impondría _____
14. él podía _____
15. habrá oído _____

16. huele _____
17. yo exponga _____
18. oyó _____
19. yo pudiera _____
20. yo haya propuesto _____
21. podrías _____
22. oigas _____
23. huelo _____
24. supondrás _____
25. puedes _____
26. Ud. oye _____
27. huelas _____
28. dispuso _____
29. yo oliera _____
30. hubieras puesto _____

Mastery Test

Write in Spanish:

1. you (s., fam.) heard _____

_____

2. we had not been able _____

_____

3. it may smell _____

4. I would not have put _____

5. you (pl., fam.) were not hearing _____

_____

6. they are imposing _____

7. I was able _____

8. does he smell? _____

9. they would hear _____

10. he may be able _____

11. I will have composed _____

_____

12. does she put? _____

13. does he hear? _____

14. you (s., fam.) will not expose _____

_____

15. they may propose _____

16. I might not be able _____

17. we might have heard _____

18. you (pl., for.) would be able _____

_____

19. they might smell _____

20. we may suppose _____

21. you (pl., fam.) will not hear _____

_____

22. are you (s., fam.) able? _____

_____

23. we might dispose _____

24. they will not put _____

25. they heard _____

26. you (pl., fam.) were able (pret) _____

_____

27. she was supposing _____

28. you (s., fam.) will be able _____

_____

29. we might not hear _____

30. did you (pl., fam.) expose? _____

_____

Querer to want, wish, love

Present Indicative: quiero, quieres, quiere, queremos, queréis, quieren I want, etc.
Imperfect: quería, etc. I was wishing, etc.
Preterit: quise, quisiste, quiso, quisimos, quisisteis, quisieron I wanted, etc.
Future: querré, querrás, querrá, querremos, querréis, querrán I shall want, etc.
Conditional: querría, etc. I would wish, etc.
Present Participle: queriendo wanting
Past Participle: querido wanted
Present Subjunctive: quiera, quieras, quiera, queramos, queráis, quieran I may want etc.
Imperfect Subjunctive: quisiera (*quisiese*), etc. I might want, etc.
Present Perfect Subjunctive: haya querido, etc. I may have wished, etc.
Pluperfect Subjunctive: hubiera (hubiese) querido, etc. I might have wished, etc.

Saber to know (a fact)

Present Indicative: sé, sabes, sabe, sabemos, sabéis, saben I know, etc.
Imperfect: sabía, etc. I was knowing, etc.
Preterit: supe, supiste, supo, supimos, supisteis, supieron, I knew, found out, etc.
Future: sabré, sabrás, sabrá, sabremos, sabréis, sabrán. I will know, etc.
Conditional: sabría, etc. I would know, etc.
Present Participle: sabiendo knowing
Past Participle: sabido known
Present Subjunctive: sepa, sepas, sepa, sepamos, sepáis, sepan I may know, etc.
Imperfect Subjunctive: supiera (*supiese*), etc. I might know, etc.
Present Perfect Subjunctive: haya sabido, etc. I may have known, etc.
Pluperfect Subjunctive: hubiera (hubiese) sabido, etc. I might have known, etc.

Salir to go out, leave

Present Indicative: salgo, sales, sale, salimos, salís, salen I go out, etc.
Imperfect: salía, etc. I was going out, etc.
Preterit: salí, etc. I went out, etc.
Future: saldré, saldrás, saldrá, saldremos, saldréis, saldrán I will go out, etc.
Conditional: saldría, etc. I would go out, etc.
Present Participle: saliendo going out
Past Participle: salido gone out
Present Subjunctive: salga, salgas, salga, salgamos, salgáis, salgan I may go out, etc.
Imperfect Subjunctive: saliera (saliese), etc. I might go out, etc.
Present Perfect Subjunctive: haya salido, etc. I may have gone out, etc.
Pluperfect Subjunctive: hubiera (hubiese) salido, etc. I might have gone out, etc.

Ser   to be

Present Indicative: *soy, eres, es, somos, sois, son*   I am, etc.

Imperfect: *era, eras, era, éramos, erais, eran*   I was, etc.

Preterit: *fui, fuiste, fue, fuimos, fuisteis, fueron*   I was, etc.

Future: seré, etc.   I will be, etc.

Conditional: sería, etc.   I would be, etc.

Present Participle: siendo   being

Past Participle: sido   been

Present Subjunctive: *sea, seas, sea, seamos, seáis, sean*   I may be, etc.

Imperfect Subjunctive: *fuera (fuese)*, etc.   I might be, etc.

Present Perfect Subjunctive: haya sido, etc.   I may have been, etc.

Pluperfect Subjuctive: hubiera (hubiese) sido, etc.   I might have been, etc.

Note: The preterits of *ser* and *ir* are identical. The context makes clear which one is intended.

Aplicación

A. Change each verb to express past time in the same person.

1. somos _____

2. sepas _____

3. salimos _____

4. sabe _____

5. eres _____

6. salga _____

7. él sea _____

8. soy _____

9. queremos _____

10. salgo _____

11. he sabido _____

12. habéis salido _____

13. quiere _____

B. Change each singular verb to plural in the same tense.

1. yo salía _____

2. Ud. sabrá _____

3. tú querrás _____

4. salió _____

5. sepas _____

6. saldrías _____

7. sabe _____

8. eres _____

9. yo había querido _____

10. salga _____

11. será _____

12. él quisiera _____

13. saldré _____

Aplicación (*cont.*)

14. estás saliendo _____

15. quieran _____

14. yo sea _____

15. Ud. fuera _____

C. Translate into English:

1. seríamos _____

2. fuimos _____

3. quisiste _____

4. habré sido _____

5. fueses _____

6. he sabido _____

7. habremos sabido _____

8. queramos _____

9. sabréis _____

10. erais _____

11. él supo _____

12. él había salido _____

13. ellos querían _____

14. sabríais _____

15. hayan salido _____

16. hubiéramos sabido _____

17. yo sea _____

18. él quisiera _____

19. salieran _____

20. supiéramos _____

Mastery Test

Write in Spanish:

1. he might know _____

2. you (pl., fam.) have gone out _____

_____

3. he would want _____

4. I was not (pret) _____

5. you (pl., fam.) have known _____

_____

6. we are _____

7. he may go out _____

8. you (s., fam.) will want _____

_____

9. we were knowing _____

10. he was (imperf.) _____

11. we were wanting _____

12. we might not go out _____

13. you (pl., fam.) will know _____

_____

14. they may be _____

15. I may have wanted _____

16. you (s., for.) will not be _____

_____

17. they will have known _____

18. they went out _____

19. you (s., fam.) had wanted _____

_____

20. we are not going out _____

21. I may have known _____

22. is he? _____

23. you (s., fam.) used to go out _____

_____

24. I did not want _____

25. they would have known _____

_____

26. don't they want _____

27. we have been _____

_____

28. he will go out _____

29. we should know _____

30. you (pl., for). might want _____

_____

31. I am going out _____

32. you (s., for.) knew _____

33. I have wanted _____

34. we might have been _____

35. you (s., fam.) may want _____

_____

36. would they go out? _____

37. I know _____

38. he might be _____

39. they were (pret) _____

40. we will have been _____

Tener   to have, hold, possess

Present Indicative: *tengo, tienes, tiene,* tenemos, tenéis, *tienen*   I have, etc.

Imperfect: tenía, etc.   I was having, etc.

Preterit: *tuve, tuviste, tuvo, tuvimos, tuvisteis, tuvieron*   I had, etc.

Future: *tendré, tendrás, tendrá, tendremos, tendréis, tendrán*   I will have, etc.

Conditional: *tendría,* etc.   I would have, etc.

Present Participle: *teniendo*   having

Past Participle: *tenido*   had

Present Subjunctive: *tenga, tengas, tenga, tengamos, tengáis, tengan*   I may have, etc.

Imperfect Subjunctive: tuviera (*tuviese*), etc.   I might have, etc.

Present Perfect Subjunctive: haya tenido, etc.   I may have had, etc.

Pluperfect Subjunctive: hubiera (hubiese) tenido, etc.   I might have had, etc.

Others:
contener   to contain
detener   to stop
mantener   to maintain
retener   to retain
sostener   to sustain

Traer   to bring

Present Indicative: *traigo*, traes, trae, etc.   I bring, etc.

Imperfect: traía, etc.   I was bringing, etc.

Preterit: *traje, trajiste, trajo, trajimos, trajisteis, trajeron*   I brought, etc.

Future: traeré, etc.   I will bring, etc.

Conditional: traería, etc.   I would bring, etc.

Present Participle: *trayendo*   bringing

Past Participle: traído   brought

Present Subjunctive: *traiga, traigas, traiga, traigamos, traigáis, traigan*   I may bring, etc.

Imperfect Subjunctive: trajera (*trajese*), etc.   I might bring, etc.

Present Perfect Subjunctive: haya traído, etc.   I may have brought, etc.

Pluperfect Subjunctive: hubiera (hubiese) traído, etc.   I might have brought, etc.

Others:
contraer   to contract

Valer   to be worth

Present Indicative: *valgo*, vales, vale, valemos, valéis, valen   I am worth, etc.

Imperfect: valía, etc.   I was worth, etc.

Preterit: valí, valiste, etc.   I was worth.

Future: *valdré, valdrás, valdrá, valdremos, valdréis, valdrán*   I will be worth

Conditional: *valdría*, etc.   I would be worth, etc.

Present Participle: valiendo   being worth

Past Participle: valido   valued

Present Subjunctive: *valga, valgas, valga, valgamos, valgáis, valgan*   I may be worth, etc.

Imperfect Subjunctive: valiera (valiese), etc.   I might be worth, etc.

Present Perfect Subjunctive: haya valido, etc.   I may have been worth, etc.

Pluperfect Subjunctive: hubiera (hubiese) valido, etc.   I might have been worth, etc.

Venir   to come

Present Indicative: *vengo, vienes, viene*, venimos, venís, *vienen*   I come, etc.

Imperfect: venía, etc.   I was coming, etc.

Preterit: *vine, viniste, vino, vinimos, vinisteis, vinieron*   I came, etc.

Future: *vendré, vendrás, vendrá, vendremos, vendréis, vendrán*   I will come, etc.
Conditional: *vendría*, etc.   I would come, etc.
Present Participle: viniendo   coming
Past Participle: venido   come
Present Subjunctive: *venga, vengas, venga, vengamos, vengáis, vengan*   I may come, etc.
Imperfect Subjunctive: *viniera* (*viniese*) etc.   I might come, etc.
Present Perfect Subjunctive: haya venido, etc.   I may have come, etc.
Pluperfect Subjunctive: hubiera (hubiese) venido, etc.   I might have come, etc.

Others:
convenir   to be suitable, agree

Para practicar

Change the infinitives to the tense and person indicated:

Present indicative **yo**

contraer	convenir	detener	mantener	sostener
_____	_____	_____	_____	_____

Present indicative **Ud.**

mantener	venir	valer	retener	traer
_____	_____	_____	_____	_____

Future **ellos**

convenir	detener	mantener	valer	sostener
_____	_____	_____	_____	_____

Preterit **él**

contener	traer	convenir	sostener	detener
_____	_____	_____	_____	_____

Present subjunctive **tú**

venir	mantener	contraer	contener	valer
_____	_____	_____	_____	_____

Imperfect subjunctive **nosotros**

contraer	venir	tener	sostener	mantener
_____	_____	_____	_____	_____

Aplicación

Write in English:

1. él habrá venido _____
2. hayas traído _____
3. ellas tuvieron _____
4. valgamos _____
5. ellos traerán _____
6. tuve _____
7. valdríamos _____
8. ellas habían venido _____
9. teníamos _____
10. traerías _____
11. has valido _____
12. vienes _____
13. valdrás _____
14. él viniera _____
15. traje _____

16. tendré _____
17. él valiera _____
18. ellos tuvieran _____
19. él ha traído _____
20. ellos vengan _____
21. ellos traían _____
22. Ud. tendría _____
23. valíamos _____
24. habremos venido _____
25. traigas _____
26. Uds. tienen _____
27. yo valdría _____
28. tuvieras _____
29. trajéramos _____
30. venías _____

Mastery Test

Write in Spanish

1. she has not come _____
2. he had had _____
3. you (s., fam.) might bring _____
4. he was worth (pret) _____
5. we might have had _____
6. they had brought _____

7. you (pl., fam.) came _____
8. he used to bring _____
9. he had _____
10. they are worth _____
11. they would not have _____
12. she brought _____

13. they were coming _____

14. do you (s., fam.) have? _____

15. they may bring _____

16. he may come _____

17. we are not bringing _____

18. we will have _____

19. you (s., fam.) will be worth _____

20. do you (pl., fam.) have? _____

21. you (s., fam.) may not bring _____

22. I am coming _____

23. you (pl., for.) may have _____

24. I am not worth _____

25. you (s., fam.) may have come _____

26. he would not bring _____

27. they had _____

28. they brought _____

29. will they come? _____

30. you (pl., fam.) might have _____

31. he might be worth _____

32. you (s., fam.) used to have _____

33. let us bring _____

34. he has had _____

35. you (s., fam.) have brought _____

36. didn't they have? _____

37. it would not be worth _____

38. you (pl., fam.) are bringing _____

39. we might come _____

40. he might bring _____

ver   to see

Present Indicative: *veo*, ves, ve, vemos, *veis*, ven   I see, etc.
Imperfect: *veía*, *veías*, *veía* *veíamos*, *veíais*, *veían*   I was seeing, etc.
Preterit: *vi*, viste, *vio*, vimos, visteis, vieron   I saw, etc.
Future: veré, etc.   I will see, etc.
Conditional: vería, etc.   I would see, etc.
Present Participle: viendo   seeing
Past Participle: *visto*   seen
Present Subjunctive: *vea*, *veas*, *vea*, *veamos*, *veáis*, *vean*   I may see, etc.
Imperfect Subjunctive: viera (viese), etc.   I might see, etc.
Present Perfect Subjunctive: haya *visto*, etc.   I may have seen, etc.
Pluperfect Subjunctive: hubiera (hubiese) *visto*   I might have seen, etc.

Irregular Past Participles

Besides the irregular verbs whose past participles have been listed previously, several verbs, otherwise regular, have irregular past participles. Common ones are:

abrir   abierto   *morir   muerto*
cubrir   cubierto   *resolver   resuelto*
escribir   escrito   *volver   vuelto*

Others:
descubrir (*descubierto*) to discover   *revolver* (*revuelto*) to stir
describir (*descrito*) to describe   *devolver* (*devuelto*) to give back, return

Aplicación

Write in English:

1. yo vea _____

2. ellos hubieran descubierto _____

_____

3. viéramos _____

4. hayas visto _____

5. verías _____

6. vimos _____

7. hemos descrito _____

8. él vea _____

9. él habrá muerto _____

10. Uds. veían _____

11. verás _____

12. yo había resuelto _____

13. vemos _____

14. viste _____

15. ellos habrían vuelto _____

Mastery Test

Write in Spanish:

1. we do not see _____

2. they were seeing _____

3. you (pl., fam.) might see _____

_____

4. he had not written _____

5. you (s., fam.) may see _____

_____

6. she did not see _____

7. have they discovered? _____

_____

8. I might have seen _____

9. we would see _____

10. he has not covered _____

11. I was seeing _____

12. she will not see _____

13. he may have seen _____

14. they would have opened _____

15. don't you (pl., fam.) see? _____

_____

Repaso de verbos irregulares

A.   Write in English:

1. él habrá venido _____

2. Uds. tuvieron _____

3. ellos irían _____

4. Ud. dirá _____

5. fuiste _____

6. él querría _____

7. vemos _____

8. fui _____

9. traje _____

10. él salía _____

11. habrás sabido _____

12. ellos estuvieran _____

13. habíamos podido _____

14. yo habría puesto _____

15. ellas den _____

16. yo ande _____

17. ellas cayeran _____

18. valgamos _____

19. él había cabido _____

20. oíste _____

21. él habrá satisfecho _____

22. él no haría _____

23. conducimos _____

24. Uds. asirían _____

25. traducías _____

26. haya habido _____

27. ella dice _____

28. vamos _____

29. habíamos sido _____

30. Uds. tendrán _____

31. ellos venían _____

32. ellas hayan visto _____

33. Uds. quisieron _____

34. él traía _____

35. ellos dieron _____

36. estés _____

37. Ud. salía _____

38. poníais _____

39. podemos _____

40. sabremos _____

41. habíamos oído _____

42. habrás valido _____

43. yo haya hecho _____

44. satisfarás _____

45. caeré _____

46. ella anduvo _____

47. él quepa _____

48. habrá _____

49. ellos tradujeron _____

50. yo conduzca _____

B.   Write in Spanish:

1. they may be (*ser*) _____

2. we will have come _____

3. you (s., fam.) were saying _____

_____

4. dos he go? _____

5. we might see _____

6. they might have _____

7. you (s., fam.) had wanted _____

_____

8. I should bring _____

9. I may know _____

10. we are (*estar*) _____

11. you (s., fam.) will have put _____

_____

12. I was able (imperf) _____

13. we have not given _____

14. he did not go out _____

15. you (pl., fam.) may have fallen _____

16. we were hearing _____

17. he fell _____

18. we would be worth _____

19. he walked _____

20. I fitted _____

21. I will not do _____

22. they used to translate _____

_____

23. they would have seized _____

_____

24. he led _____

25. you (s., fam.) may deduce _____

_____

26. there would be _____

27. he will have said _____

28. I would go _____

29. they may have seen _____

30. they may have _____

31. he was coming _____

32. she was wanting _____

33. you (pl., fam.) have been (ser) _____

_____

34. let us not bring _____

35. he doesn't know _____

36. you (s., fam.) could (pret) _____

_____

37. we will be (estar) _____

38. give! (pl.) _____

39. I would go out _____

40. you (pl., fam.) will put _____

_____

41. I may hear _____

42. we will not walk _____

43. I will fit _____

44. you (s., for.) have been worth _____

_____

45. we might satisfy _____

46. we did not do _____

47. I am falling _____

48. we may seize _____

49. they might have been (ser) _____

_____

50. he might lead _____

Repaso general 2

A. Write in English:

1. pensamos _____

2. Ud. abrió _____

3. pierdan _____

4. ella contesta _____

5. entiendo _____

6. llegué _____

7. Ud. dirá _____

8. él se divirtió _____

9. yo duermo _____

10. trajimos _____

11. hice _____

12. ellos vendrán _____

124

13. sepas _____

14. yo pusiera _____

15. podamos _____

16. Ud. escoja _____

17. volviéramos _____

18. ellos saquen _____

19. ellos distinguen _____

20. yo buscara _____

21. leeré _____

22. Uds. conocerían _____

23. ellos tendrán _____

24. di _____

25. verás _____

26. él insinúa _____

27. yo empiece _____

28. enviamos _____

29. yo haya jugado _____

30. yo confíe _____

B. Write in Spanish:

1. we were writing _____

2. he understands _____

3. they live _____

4. they were traveling _____

5. you (s., fam.) keep _____

6. you were bringing _____

7. do we say? _____

8. he wants _____

9. he dressed himself _____

10. they did not see _____

11. we went out _____

12. he might put _____

13. they have not done _____

14. I don't know (*saber*) _____

15. you (s., fam.) could (pret) _____

_____

16. we directed _____

17. I looked for _____

18. they might choose _____

19. explain! (pl., for.) _____

20. he may arrive _____

21. you are worth _____

22. did they read? _____

23. you (s., fam.) might give _____

_____

24. let's not go _____

25. he may have _____

26. they may play _____

27. I denied _____

28. he may continue _____

29. I did not begin _____

30. they may send _____

Repaso general 3

A. Write in English:

1. empecé _____

2. yo juegue _____

3. negábamos _____

4. ella continúa _____

5. ellos enviarán _____

6. Ud. consigue _____

7. tuve _____

8. condujiste _____

9. yo salía _____

10. supieron _____

11. él oiría _____

12. Ud. cabe _____

13. él ponga _____

14. podríamos _____

15. vengo _____

16. ellos habrán muerto _____

17. yo reía _____

18. él contribuía _____

19. él destruye _____

20. Ud. poseía _____

21. construyan _____

22. él pierde _____

23. servíamos _____

24. él conocía _____

25. ella hirió _____

26. yo piense _____

27. echaron _____

28. él habrá perdido _____

29. escuchabas _____

30. ella había vuelto _____

B. Write in Spanish:

1. you (pl, fam.) were playing _____

_____

2. they might begin _____

3. I continue _____

4. I may trust _____

5. they do not read _____

6. he did not want _____

7. they would be (ser) _____

8. I am not correcting _____

9. I went _____

10. he said _____

11. I may see _____

12. you (s., for.) were falling _____

_____

13. I did _____

14. I have put _____

15. they will go out _____

16. I may read _____

17. we had slept _____

18. we might laugh _____

19. he may die _____

20. they did not believe _____

21. I sent _____

22. do you (pl., fam.) consent? _____

_____

23. they may destroy _____

24. he was repeating _____

25. we used to lose _____

26. you (s., fam.) do not return _____

_____

27. we were spending _____

28. I was living _____

29. you (pl., fam.) understood _____

_____

30. they have opened _____

Answer Key

Para practicar

PRESENT

pp. 2–5

(1) acabo	(2) tomo	(1) vendo	(2) bebo	(1) vivo	(2) recibo
acabas	tomas	vendes	bebes	vives	recibes
acaba	toma	vende	bebe	vive	recibe
acaba	toma	vende	bebe	vive	recibe
acabamos	tomamos	vendemos	bebemos	vivimos	recibimos
acabáis	tomáis	vendéis	bebéis	vivís	recibís
acaban	toman	venden	beben	viven	reciben
acaban	toman	venden	bebenl	viven	reciben

estudio, comprendo, temo, necesito, parto, enseño, vendo.

hablas, asistes, abres, bebes, preguntas, tomas, escuchas.

contesta, abre, aprende, entra, lee, vive, come.

escribe, estudia, acaba, teme, parte, comprende, vende.

aprendemos, asistimos, tomamos, escuchamos, hablamos, vivimos, tememos.

habláis, asistís, bebéis, leéis, tomáis, lleváis, enseñáis.

comen, escriben, necesitan, entran, acaban, leen, viven.

temen, llevan, estudian, preguntan, contestan, comprenden, parten.

Aplicación

pp. 5–6

A.
1. tomamos
2. aprende
3. venden
4. asisto
5. contestas
6. bebe
7. abrimos
8. necesita
9. tomáis
10. lee
11. aprendo
12. tememos
13. recibís
14. escriben
15. abre
16. enseñamos
17. contesto
18. estudiamos
19. abro
20. toma
21. pregunta
22. leen
23. reciben
24. temes
25. leemos

Aplicación (*cont.*)

B.
1. escribimos,
   we write
2. ellos contestan,
   they answer
3. vivimos,
   we live
4. Uds. necesitan,
   you need
5. ellos beben,
   they drink
6. aprendéis,
   you learn
7. ellos venden,
   they sell
8. asistimos,
   we attend
9. Uds. enseñan,
   you teach
10. abrís,
    you open
11. Uds. comprenden,
    you understand
12. ellas escuchan,
    they listen
13. teméis,
    you fear
14. ellas preguntan,
    they ask
15. Uds. leen,
    you read
16. tomamos,
    we take
17. recibimos,
    we receive
18. ellos estudian,
    they study
19. necesitamos,
    we need
20. escribís,
    you write

Mastery Test

pp. 6−7

1. contestamos
2. vendéis
3. él pregunta
4. ellos venden
5. no necesitamos
6. estudiamos
7. aprendo
8. ¿escuchan ellos?
9. él no lee
10. Ud. no entra
11. trabajamos
12. ¿escribes?
13. ellos preguntan
14. Uds. toman
15. vendo
16. ella no trabaja
17. ellos no creen
18. ellos esconden
19. él escribe
20. ¿temes?
21. vivimos
22. él enseña
23. ella teme
24. recibís
25. él abre
26. ellos no toman
27. asistimos
28. ¿vende él?
29. estudio
30. creo
31. ellos unen
32. ellos no abren
33. enseñas
34. él asiste
35. preguntamos
36. ¿aprenden Uds?
37. ella bebe
38. ¿estudias?
39. Ud. vive
40. ellos entran

IMPERFECT

Para practicar

pp. 8−10

tomaba, metía, vivía, compraba, sentía, viajaba, corría.

aprendías, subías, pasabas, guardabas, cosías, esperabas, acababas.

tocaba, amaba, sabía, jugaba, viajaba, comprendía, escribía.

echaba, preparaba, leía, vivía, abría, corría, trabajaba.

estudiábamos, vendíamos, subíamos, comprendíamos, abríamos, preparábamos, tomábamos.

escribíais, trabajabais, comíais, bebíais, recibíais, comprabais, llevabais.

pasaban, caminaban, respondían, subían, hablaban, abrían, sacaban.

acababan, salían, contestaban, vivían, guardaban, corrían, viajaban.

Aplicación

pp. 10−11

A.
1. hablaba
2. vivíamos
3. sabía
4. conocían
5. pedían
6. corríamos
7. partías
8. pasaba
9. esperabais
10. acababan
11. caminaba
12. comprendía
13. tomaban
14. escribía
15. amaba
16. conocíais
17. bebías
18. comprábamos
19. subían
20. corría
21. respondía
22. guardabas
23. aprendía
24. llevaban
25. pasabais

1. contestábamos, we were answering
2. vendías, you were selling
3. preguntaba, he was asking
4. aprendía, I was learning
5. escuchaban, they were listening
6. Ud. escribía, you were writing
7. aprendían, they were learning
8. Ud. estudiaba, you were studying
9. vivíamos, we were living
10. temía, he was fearing
11. abría, he was opening
12. enseñaban, they were teaching
13. asistía, he was attending
14. tomábamos, we were taking
15. leía, I was reading
16. Uds. bebían, you were drinking
17. temía, I was fearing
18. recibían, they were receiving
19. necesitaba, I was needing
20. Uds. vivían, you were living
21. abríamos, we were opening
22. contestabais, you were answering
23. tomabas, you were taking
24. bebía, he was drinking
25. abríais, you were opening

Mastery Test

pp. 11−12

1. vivían
2. trabajábamos
3. no vendías
4. vivíamos
5. no necesitaban
6. Ud. aprendía
7. creía
8. preguntabais
9. temía
10. ¿comprendías?
11. enseñaba
12. Uds. tomaban
13. no escuchábamos
14. vendía
15. Uds. abrían
16. ¿recibían?
17. asistíamos
18. estudiabas
19. leía
20. vivían
21. Uds. no escondían
22. recibía
23. no comprendían
24. comía
25. Ud. vendía
26. no tomabas
27. escuchaban
28. ¿asistía?
29. necesitabais
30. contestaba

PRETERIT

Para practicar

pp. 13—15

viajé, trabajé, estudié, comí, vendí, insistí, recibí.

uniste, acabaste, compraste, rompiste, corriste, abriste, tomaste.

comió, asistió, echó, preparó, subió, pasó, trabajó.

viajó, habló, aprendió, resistió, llamó, respondió, echó.

trabajamos, compramos, amamos, vendimos, bebimos, corrimos, vivimos.

estudiasteis, comisteis, abristeis, tomasteis, viajasteis, subisteis, pasasteis.

trabajaron, compraron, hablaron, aprendieron, temieron, escribieron, viajaron.

guardaron, comprendieron, asistieron, abrieron, pasaron, echaron, bebieron.

Aplicación

pp. 15—16

A.
1. llevé
2. abrimos
3. llegaste
4. comieron
5. bebió
6. metisteis
7. viajaron
8. vivió
9. pasaron
10. vendieron
11. abrí
12. asistió
13. recibieron
14. tomamos
15. temisteis
16. abrió
17. escribieron
18. necesitaron
19. vendiste
20. bebimos
21. aprendieron
22. tomé
23. estudió
24. bebió
25. recibí

B.
1. tomamos, tomábamos
2. enseñaron, enseñaban
3. contestó, contestaba
4. recibieron, recibían
5. aprendió, aprendía
6. asistí, asistía
7. temimos, temíamos
8. vendieron, vendían
9. aprendí, aprendía
10. contesté, contestaba
11. tomaron, tomaban
12. abrió, abría
13. necesitó, necesitaba
14. recibiste, recibías
15. trabajó, trabajaba
16. echaron, echaban
17. subieron, subían
18. comprendí, comprendía
19. corrió, corría
20. trabajé, trabajaba
21. preparó, preparaba
22. guardaron, guardaban
23. pasamos, pasábamos
24. viajé, viajaba
25. echaste, echabas

Mastery Test

pp. 16–17

1. contestamos
2. vendieron
3. aprendí
4. ¿escuchaste?
5. no preguntó
6. Ud. escondió
7. tomamos
8. no bebieron
9. asistimos
10. enseñé
11. preguntaste
12. trabajaron
13. Uds. unieron
14. viví
15. contestasteis
16. Uds. escribieron
17. comprendió
18. no aprendieron
19. escribimos
20. ¿estudió?
21. vendiste
22. enseñó
23. asistió
24. vendí
25. vivíais
26. recibieron
27. asistí
28. preguntaron
29. bebimos
30. Ud. estudió
31. no contesté
32. ¿abrieron Uds.?
33. no comprendieron
34. no necesitaste
35. vendimos
36. ¿tomó Ud.?
37. no recibimos
38. temió
39. escribí
40. ¿preguntasteis?

Repaso (Present, imperfect, preterit)

pp. 18–19

1. vivían
2. abría
3. no trabajaron
4. subíamos
5. comprendo
6. no tomaron
7. corría
8. contestaron
9. trabajo
10. preparaste
11. Uds. estudiaban
12. guardan
13. pasábamos
14. viajé
15. Ud. necesita
16. no vivía
17. Uds. abrían
18. escribía
19. subo
20. comprendió
21. escribía
22. respondes
23. comprendimos
24. no aprendisteis
25. preparan
26. aprendemos
27. corrimos
28. Uds. pasaban
29. trabajaron
30. asistimos
31. no escribíamos
32. eché
33. estudiábamos
34. trabajé
35. vivíamos
36. guardamos
37. comprendiste
38. asistieron
39. vendíamos
40. paso
41. viví
42. temes
43. escuchó
44. no guardasteis
45. bebe
46. guardaban
47. partió
48. Ud. temió
49. subimos
50. no contesto

FUTURE

Para practicar

pp. 20−22

compraré, hablaré, leeré, viviré, sentiré, seré, asistiré.

estudiarás, encontrarás, correrás, tomarás, venderás, conocerás, partirás.

enseñará, perderá, dormirá, aprenderá, recibirá, abrirá, necesitará.

dudará, creerá, amará, escribirá, guardará, correrá, subirá.

contestaremos, temeremos, preguntaremos, subiremos, viajaremos, aprenderemos, viviremos.

prepararéis, echaréis, contestaréis, trabajaréis, viajaréis, responderéis, amaréis.

comprarán, leerán, sentirán, recibirán, decidirán, andarán, pasarán.

prepararán, aprenderán, echarán, viajarán, contestarán, correrán, marcharán.

Aplicación

pp. 22−23

A.
1. hablará
2. estaremos
3. será
4. encontrarán
5. leerá
6. dudaré
7. perderemos
8. enseñarás
9. dormiréis
10. andará
11. decidirás
12. compraré
13. vivirá
14. sentirá
15. beberá
16. estudiaréis
17. abrirá
18. venderás
19. escucharán
20. aprenderán
21. necesitará
22. contestará
23. temeremos
24. tomaré
25. recibirás

B.
1. vivirán
   they will live
2. abriré
   I will open
3. subiremos,
   we will go up
4. comprenderás
   you will understand
5. aprenderemos,
   we will learn
6. trabajarán
   they will work
7. Ud. correrá,
   you will run
8. contestarán,
   they will answer
9. trabajaré,
   I will work
10. prepararéis,
    you will prepare
11. pasaremos,
    we will spend
12. viajaré,
    I will travel
13. echarás,
    you will throw
14. partiré,
    I will leave
15. abrirás,
    you will open

16. Uds. escribirán,
    you will write
17. subiré,
    I will go up
18. comprenderá,
    she will understand
19. correremos,
    we will run
20. Ud. contestará,
    you will answer

21. tomaremos,
    we will take
22. enseñarán,
    they will teach
23. acabarás,
    you will finish
24. trabajará,
    he will work
25. escribiré
    I will write

Mastery Test

pp. 24−25

1. adornarás
2. admiraba
3. ofenderéis
4. molesta
5. Uds. discutirán
6. insistí
7. discutirá
8. emprenderemos
9. limpiarán
10. Uds. llaman
11. admiraré
12. adornó
13. molestas
14. discutiré
15. insistieron
16. cubrían
17. cubriremos
18. admiramos
19. Uds. emprendieron
20. insistimos

21. discutieron
22. limpiaremos
23. limpiaba
24. decidí
25. llama
26. ofendíamos
27. llamaremos
28. Ud. discutió
29. no admiraremos
30. no llaman
31. decidís
32. cubrí
33. Ud. no discutirá
34. no decidiremos
35. ¿limpiarás?
36. no insistiréis
37. cubrirán
38. Uds. limpiaron
39. insistíamos
40. ofendió

CONDITIONAL

Para practicar

pp. 26−28

admiraría, decidiría, trabajaría, viviría, bebería, abriría, moriría.

adornarías, ofenderías, responderías, estudiarías, venderías, escribirías, sentirías.

molestaría, emprendería, correría, necesitaría, aprendería. llevaría, partiría.

Para practicar (*cont.*)

llamaría, echaría, aprendería, contestaría, temería, sacaría, hablaría.

limpiaríamos, viajaríamos, comprenderíamos, preguntaríamos, leeríamos, tocaríamos, comeríamos.

cubriríais, pasaríais, subiríais, enseñaríais, creeríais, conoceríais, meteríais.

discutirían, guardarían, abrirían, escucharían, recibirían, traerían, pedirían.

insistirían, prepararían, escribirían, tomarían, asistirían, dormirían, rogarían.

Aplicación

pp. 28–29

A. 1. admirarían
    2. discutiría
    3. cubrirías
    4. limpiaría
    5. venderíais
    6. preguntaría
    7. venderían
    8. estudiaríamos
    9. viviríamos
    10. temería
    11. abriría
    12. tomarían
    13. escribiríamos
    14. contestarían
    15. temerían
    16. llevarías
    17. bebería
    18. aprendería
    19. echaría
    20. viajarían
    21. necesitaríais
    22. escucharían
    23. enseñaríamos
    24. asistirían
    25. recibirías

B. a) 1. contestaríamos, we should answer
    2. aprendería, I should learn
    3. escucharían, they should listen
    4. leería, he should read
    5. esconderíamos, we should hide
    6. escribiríais, you should write
    7. estudiarían, you should study
    8. vendería, I should sell
    9. enseñaría, she should teach
    10. comprenderían, they should understand

b) 1. vivirían, you should live
    2. abriría, he should open
    3. trabajarían, they should work
    4. subiríamos, we should go up
    5. comprendería, he should understand
    6. aprenderíais, you should learn
    7. correría, he should run
    8. prepararías, you should prepare
    9. guardaríamos, we should keep
    10. viajaría, she should travel

Mastery Test

pp. 29–30

    1. decidirás
    2. molestaría
    3. Ud. adornaba
    4. ¿ofendería?
    5. insistí
    6. discutiríamos

    7. admiraron
    8. no adornaría
    9. ofenderé
    10. ofendían
    11. ¿limpiaría?
    12. emprenden

13. admirarían
14. limpiaré
15. Uds. molestarían
16. no cubriremos
17. cubre
18. decidirían
19. ¿admirarás?
20. admiramos
21. insistían

22. no insistiría
23. Uds. limpiaron
24. decidiría
25. insistirás
26. ¿llamarían?
27. cubriríais
28. molestaremos
29. no ofenderían
30. ¿decidiré?

PROGRESSIVE TENSES

Para practicar

pp. 26—28

admirando, adornando, subiendo, cubriendo, acabando, corriendo, respondiendo, tomando, sacando, decidiendo, dando.

estoy abriendo, estoy llevando, estoy perdiendo, estoy buscando, estoy estudiando, estoy bebiendo.

estás viviendo, estás aprendiendo, estás tomando, estás escribiendo, estás trabajando, estás enseñando.

están vendiendo, están abriendo, están contestando, están asistiendo, están escuchando, están entrando.

estamos recibiendo, estamos echando, estamos admirando, estamos pasando, estamos respondiendo, estamos corriendo.

Aplicación

pp. 32—33

A.
1. estaba llevando
2. estabas estudiando
3. estabais trabajando
4. estábamos subiendo
5. estaban corriendo
6. estaba escuchando
7. estaban jugando
8. estábamos escribiendo
9. estabas comiendo
10. estaba partiendo
11. estábamos tomando
12. estaban acabando
13. estaba respondiendo
14. estaban decidendo
15. estaba cubriendo

B.
1. están recibiendo
2. estamos trabajando
3. estáis abriendo
4. estáis preguntando
5. no está escuchando
6. estamos viviendo
7. está bebiendo
8. están asistiendo
9. estás vendiendo
10. no está tomando
11. está enseñando
12. estáis contestando
13. está estudiando
14. no está comiendo
15. estoy aprendiendo

Mastery Test

pp. 33–34

1. admiraba,	estaba admirando
2. decides,	estás decidiendo
3. limpiaba,	estaba limpiando
4. insistían,	estaban insistiendo
5. no preparan,	no están preparando
6. Ud. llama,	Ud. está llamando
7. cubrían,	estaban cubriendo
8. ¿adornaban Uds.?,	¿estaban adornando Uds.?
9. bebe,	está bebiendo
10. vivíamos,	estábamos viviendo
11. no escribías,	no estabas escribiendo
12. paso,	estoy pasando
13. estudian,	están estudiando
14. pasábamos,	estábamos pasando
15. ¿subís?	¿estáis subiendo?
16. abría,	estaba abriendo
17. ¿corría?,	¿estaba corriendo?
18. no vivía,	no estaba viviendo
19. no escribimos,	no estamos escribiendo

Repaso (Future, conditional progressive)

pp. 34–35

1. Uds. asistirán
2. estaba admirando
3. ofenderás
4. molestaría
5. estáis buscando
6. Ud. no discutiría
7. estaba insistiendo
8. está estudiando
9. subiré
10. admiraría
11. estaban respondiendo
12. no está molestando
13. ¿discutirán?
14. estaba trabajando
15. no estás corriendo
16. escuchará
17. estaba entrando
18. estamos pasando
19. cubriríamos
20. estaban limpiando
21. no abriré
22. no perderíais
23. Ud. está llamando
24. limpiará
25. enseñarás
26. estáis trabajando
27. echará
28. estaba escribiendo
29. están bebiendo
30. admiraría
31. estábamos llamando
32. estaba discutiendo
33. admiraré
34. Ud. molestaría
35. pasarán
36. Uds. escribirían
37. estaban decidiendo
38. responderá

PERFECT TENSES

pp. 36–37

tú habías hablado, Ud. había hablado, él había hablado, nosotros habíamos hablado, vosotros habíais hablado, Uds. habían hablado, ellos habían hablado.

yo habré comido, tú habrás comido, Ud. habrá comido, él habrá comido, nosotros habremos comido, vosotros habréis comido, Uds. habrán comido, ellos habrán comido.

I will have eaten, you will have eaten, he will have eaten, we will have eaten, you will have eaten, they will have eaten.

yo habría partido, tú habrías partido, Ud. habría, partido, él habría partido, nosotros habríamos partido, vosotros habríais partido, Uds. habrían partido, ellos habrían partido.

I would have left, you would have left, he would have left, we would have left, you would have left, they would have left.

Para practicar

pp. 37–38

1. he aprendido,	había aprendido,	habré aprendido,	habría aprendido
2. han limpiado,	habían limpiado,	habrán limpiado,	habrían limpiado
3. ha vivido,	había vivido	habrá vivido,	habría vivido
4. hemos comprado,	habíamos comprado,	habremos comprado,	habríamos comprado
5. has asistido,	habías asistido,	habrás asistido,	habrías asistido
6. han vendido,	habían vendido,	habrán vendido,	habrían vendido
7. hemos tomado,	habíamos tomado,	habremos tomado,	habríamos tomado
8. ha aprendido,	había aprendido,	habrá aprendido,	habría aprendido
9. ha bebido,	había bebido,	habrá bebido,	habría bedido
10. ha contestado,	había contestado,	habrá contestado,	habría contestado
11. habéis recibido,	habíais recibido,	habréis recibido,	habríais recibido
12. han preparado,	habían preparado,	habrán preparado,	habrían preparado
13. hemos enseñado,	habíamos enseñado,	habremos enseñado,	habríamos enseñado
14. has temido,	habías temido,	habrás temido,	habrías temido
15. ha preguntado,	había preguntado,	habrá preguntado,	habría preguntado
16. han estudiado,	habían estudiado,	habrán estudiado,	habrían estudiado
17. ha pasado,	había pasado,	habrá pasado,	habría pasado
18. hemos subido,	habíamos subido,	habremos subido,	habríamos subido
19. han salido,	habían salido,	habrán salido,	habrían salido
20. has guardado,	habías guardado,	habrás guardado,	habrías guardado
21. he esperado,	había esperado,	habré esperado,	habría esperado
22. habéis trabajado,	habíais trabajado,	habréis trabajado,	habríais trabajado
23. han vivido,	habían vivido,	habrán vivido,	habrían vivido
24. ha partido,	había partido,	habrá partido,	habría partido
25. ha acabado,	había acabado,	habrá acabado,	habría acabado

Aplicación

p. 39

1. Ud. ha comprendido
2. habías vendido
3. habían escuchado
4. habrán subido
5. ha preguntado
6. Ud. habrá discutido
7. habían aprendido
8. Ud. había estudiado
9. has escrito
10. habremos guardado
11. habrían admirado
12. habréis echado
13. habías temido
14. he asistido
15. habíamos tomado
16. habrías preparado
17. había bebido
18. habremos vivido
19. hemos corrido
20. habrá viajado
21. habrías decidido
22. habíais contestado
23. habíais partido
24. habré limpiado
25. habríais molestado

Mastery Test

pp. 39–40

1. habré aprendido
2. había limpiado
3. hemos comprado
4. habían vivido
5. habría corrido
6. he preguntado
7. habrás recibido
8. habías temido
9. ha asistido
10. habrían vendido
11. habremos tomado
12. Ud. ha contestado
13. he necesitado
14. Uds. habrían preguntado
15. han pasado
16. habrás discutido
17. han recibido
18. habría decidido
19. habrán escuchado
20. habremos entrado
21. Ud. habría asistido
22. habríais comprendido
23. hemos vivido
24. Uds. habrán trabajado
25. había tomado

Repaso (Indicative tenses)

pp. 40–41

1. contestas
2. vivían
3. estaba abriendo
4. estáis vendiendo
5. admiraré
6. trabajaron
7. pregunta
8. Uds. no ofenderán
9. subíamos
10. no venden
11. molestaría
12. estaba comprendiendo
13. estudiamos
14. ¿estáis adornando?
15. Uds. estaban aprendiendo
16. no vivimos
17. Ud. discute
18. estaba corriendo

19. ¿necesita?
20. molestaron
21. no contestaron
22. teme
23. insistimos
24. trabajé
25. echaré
26. preparabais
27. abre
28. Ud. estaba admirando
29. guardaron
30. ofenderé
31. estábamos pasando
32. adornaría
33. limpiaremos
34. escribimos

35. estaban cubriendo
36. Uds. estaban echando
37. temerán
38. estaba viviendo
39. viajaba
40. estudias
41. Uds. están llamando
42. abriríais
43. bebo
44. estábamos insistiendo
45. escribías
46. ¿llamarán?
47. subí
48. no discutirían
49. comprendió
50. viven

PRESENT SUBJUNCTIVE

Para practicar

pp. 42–44

eche, aprenda, moleste, emprenda, comprenda, asista, viva.

viajes, comprendas, llames, estudies, bebas, abras, escribas.

pase, suba, limpie, necesite, venda, escriba, prepare.

guarde, abra, cubra, conteste, aprenda, llame, tome.

preparemos, escribamos, discutamos, preguntemos, temamos, trabajemos, unamos.

trabajéis, viváis, insistáis, enseñéis, leáis, paséis, temáis.

respondan, admiren, decidan, escuchen, vivan, guarden, viajen.

corran, adornen, ofendan, tomen, reciban, echen, suban.

Aplicación

p. 44

1. lleve
2. viva
3. escriban
4. trabajéis
5. lean
6. hable
7. Ud. estudie
8. llamemos
9. viajes
10. abra
11. creamos
12. mande
13. escribas

14. tomemos
15. comprendan
16. coma
17. vivas
18. asista
19. Ud. note
20. caminen
21. meta
22. observéis
23. partáis
24. andes
25. insistamos

Mastery Test

pp. 44–45

1. no comprenda
2. ¡corra! ¡corran!
3. pregunte
4. estudie
5. beban
6. venda
7. estudien
8. no venda
9. ¡beba! ¡beban!
10. comprendamos
11. reciba
12. vendan
13. estudiéis

14. ¡no preguntes!
15. no corramos
16. recibas
17. enseñe
18. comprendáis
19. llamemos
20. abra
21. ¡escriba! ¡escriban!
22. viaje
23. tomes
24. Ud. viva
25. insistamos

IMPERFECT SUBJUNCTIVE

Para practicar

pp. 46–47

temiera, asistiera, abriera, acabara, escuchara, necesitara.

estudiara, abriera, aprendiera, tuviera, hablara, enseñara.

comprendiéramos, comiéramos, entráramos, partiéramos, viviéramos, metiéramos.

partieses, preguntases, vivieses, vendieses, hablases, guardases.

enseñase, tomase, comiese, aprendiese, asistiese, pasase.

hablasen, contestasen, estudiasen, tomasen, leyesen, escribiesen.

Aplicación

pp. 47–48

A.
1. hablara, hablase
2. viviéramos, viviésemos
3. corriéramos, corriésemos
4. partieras, partieses
5. pasara, pasase
6. esperarais, esperaseis
7. acabaran, acabasen
8. caminaran, caminasen
9. comprendiera, comprendiese
10. tomaran, tomasen
11. escribiera, escribiese
12. amara, amase

B.
1. contestáramos, contestásemos
2. vendieras, vendieses
3. preguntara, preguntase
4. aprendiera, aprendiese
5. escucharan, escuchasen
6. Ud. escribiera, escribiese
7. apendiera, aprendiese
8. Ud. estudiara, estudiese
9. viviéramos, viviésemos
10. temiera, temiese
11. abriera, abriese
12. enseñaran, enseñasen

13. bebieras, bebieses
14. compráramos, comprásemos
15. subieran, subiesen

13. asistiera, asistiese
14. tomáramos, tomásemos
15. Uds. recibieran, recibiesen

Mastery Test

p. 48

1. enseñara, enseñase
2. vivieran, viviesen
3. subiéramos, subiésemos
4. no comprendiera, no comprendiese
5. tomaran, tomasen
6. corriera, corriese
7. contestaras, contestases
8. trabajara, trabajases
9. no prepararais, preparaseis
10. Ud. estudiara, estudiase

11. guardaran, guardasen
12. no pasáramos, pasásemos
13. viajara, viajase
14. necesitaras, necesitases
15. no viviera, viviese
16. abrierais, abrieseis
17. escribiera, escribiese
18. Uds. respondieran, repondiesen
19. temiera, temiese
20. comieran, comiesen

PERFECT TENSES OF THE SUBJUNCTIVE

Para practicar

p. 50

haya estudiado, haya necesitado, haya viajado,
hayamos pasado, hayas tomado, hayan vendido,
hayáis asistido, hayan llamado, hubiera (hubiese) vivido, hubieran (hubiesen) guardado, hubieras (hubieses) caminado,
hubieran (hubiesen) bebido, hubiéramos (hubiésemos) echado,
hubierais (hubieseis) asistido, hubiera (hubiese) aprendido

Aplicación

pp. 50–51

1. haya escuchado
2. hubiéramos (hubiésemos) vivido
3. hubieran (hubiesen) guardado
4. hayan trabajado
5. hayamos comprendido
6. hubiéramos (hubiésemos) vivido
7. hubieras (hubieses) subido
8. haya comprendido
9. no hubiera (hubiese) tomado
10. Ud. haya corrido
11. hubieran (hubiesen) respondido
12. hayas preparado
13. hubieras (hubiese) estudiado

14. hayamos pasado
15. hayáis viajado
16. Uds. hayan necesitado
17. haya subido
18. hubiera (hubiese) partido
19. no hayas aprendido
20. no haya contestado
21. hubieras (hubieses) temido
22. hubieran (hubiesen) asistido
23. no haya vivido
24. hubieras (hubieses) discutido
25. hayáis llamado

Mastery Test

p. 51

1. haya aprendido
2. hubiera (hubiese) tomado
3. hubiera (hubiese) limpiado
4. hayas trabajado
5. hayamos comprado
6. hubiéramos (hubiésemos) vivido
7. hubieran (hubiesen) recibido
8. hubierais (hubieses) comprendido
9. hubiera (hubiese) asistido
10. hayamos tomado
11. haya necesitado
12. Ud. hubiera (hubiese) preguntado
13. hayan vivido
14. hubiera (hubiese) corrido
15. hayamos entrado
16. hubiera (hubiese) preguntado
17. hayan escuchado
18. hayáis temido
19. haya decidido
20. Uds. hubieran (hubiesen) contestado

Repaso del subjuntivo

pp. 52–53

1. comprenda
2. hayáis bebido
3. hubiéramos (hubiésemos) comprendido
4. no reciba
5. enseñara (enseñase)
6. corriéramos (corriésemos)
7. Ud. hubiera (hubiese) recibido
8. comprendas
9. no comprendiéramos (comprendiésemos)
10. haya estudiado
11. no corriera (corriese)
12. hayamos enseñado
13. hayan vendido
14. hubieran (hubiesen) bebido
15. ho haya recibido
16. hubiera (hubiese) recibido
17. comprendamos
18. haya bebido
19. ¡estudie!
20. hubiéramos (hubiésemos) recibido
21. venda
22. comprendieran, comprendiesen
23. hayamos estudiado
24. ho estudiéis
25. estudiara, estudiase
26. haya preguntado
27. hayas vendído
28. hubierais (hubieseis) bebido
29. no hubiera (hubiese) enseñado
30. estudiemos
31. ¡no vendáis!
32. comprendiera, comprendiese
33. haya estudiado
34. hubiera (hubiese) bebido
35. hubieran (hubiesen) enseñado
36. no preguntemos
37. bebieran, bebiesen
38. !corran!
39. corrieran, corriesen
40. Uds. hayan estudiado

REFLEXIVE VERBS

pp. 54–55

te levantabas, Ud. se levantaba, él se levantaba, nosotros nos levantábamos, vosotros os leventabais, Uds. se levantaban, ellos se levantaban.

te levantaste, Ud. se levantó, él se levantó, nos levantamos, os levantasteis, Uds. se levantaron, ellos se levantaron.

te levantarás, Ud. se levantará, él se levantará, nos levantaremos, os levantaréis, Uds. se levantarán, ellos se levantarán.

te levantarias, Ud. se levantaría, él se levantaría, nos levantaríamos, os levantaríais, Uds. se levantarían, ellos se levantarían.

me estaba levantando, estaba levantándome; I was getting up

(1) me había levantado (2) me habre levantado (3) me habría levantado

(1) I had gotten up (2) I will have gotten up (3) I would have gotten up

te levantes, Ud. se levante, él se levante, nos levantemos, os levantéis, Uds. se levanten, ellos se levanten

te levantaras, se levantara, se levantara, nos levantáramos, os levantarais, Uds. se levantaran, ellos se levantaran

te levantases, se levantase, se levantase, nos levantásemos, os levantaseis, Uds. se levantasen, ellos se levantasen

PRESENT PERFECT

p. 56

me haya levantado, te hayas levantado, se haya levantado, se haya levantado

I may have gotten up, you may have gotten up, you may have gotten up, he may have gotten up

nos hubiésemos levantado, os hubieseis levantado, se hubiesen levantado, se hubiesen levantado

we might have gotten up, you might have gotten up, you might have gotten up, they might have gotten up

Aplicación

pp. 56−57

A. 1. os lavéis
    2. se peinaban
    3. se levantó
    4. nos peinemos
    5. nos levantábamos
    6. se lavan
    7. nos levantamos
    8. se hayan peinado
    9. te lavabas
    10. me peiné
    11. os levantáis

B. 1. se hayan levantado
    2. nos hemos levantado
    3. te has peinado
    4. os habéis levantado
    5. nos habremos peinado
    6. me había peinado
    7. se había levantado
    8. nos habríamos levantado
    9. se habían peinado
    10. se haya lavado
    11. os hayáis peinado

144

Aplicación (*cont.*)

12. te hubieras levantado
13. se peina
14. me lavaré
15. te peinarías

12. nos hayamos lavado
13. me haya levantado
14. se habrán levantado
15. me habré lavado

Mastery Test

1. se haya lavado
2. se estaban lavando (estaban lavándose)
3. se peinan
4. se lavara (lavase)
5. me había levantado
6. se levantaron
7. se habrán lavado
8. me estoy peinando (estoy peinándome)
9. se habrían levantado
10. me levantaba

11. me lavo
12. se levante
13. nos lavaremos
14. se ha lavado
15. nos peináramos (peinásemos)
16. se lavaron
17. me lavaría
18. se levantan
19. te lavaste
20. se hubieran (hubiesen) lavado

Repaso de verbos regulares

pp. 58–61

A.
1. acabamos
2. comprendisteis
3. ellos temían
4. necesitaremos
5. partiríais
6. estamos enseñando
7. partís
8. Uds. hablen
9. han enseñado
10. hayáis hablado
11. estaban lavándose
12. habíais vendido
13. ellos hubiesen asistido
14. bebierais
15. habrán preguntado
16. habríais tomado
17. escuchan
18. hemos estudiado
19. habréis temido
20. aprenderán
21. comprendáis
22. están viviendo
23. Uds. habían acabado
24. contestamos
25. Uds. vendiesen
26. habríamos partido
27. abríais
28. Uds. entrarían
29. estabais comiendo
30. Uds. hayan tomado

B.
1. I leave
2. you wrote
3. you will attend
4. they used to live
5. we would take
6. you taught
7. he is studying
8. we will fear
9. you were opening
10. she would sell
11. you have attended
12. you have eaten

13. they had understood
14. you are listening
15. we will have had
16. I had studied
17. I was getting up
18. you will have spoken
19. we might drink
20. you would have answered
21. you may eat

22. he may write
23. he may have washed
24. we might learn
25. you might have studied
26. you may have spoken
27. you might have eaten
28. they fear
29. you would have carried
30. you used to carry

C. 1. temen
 2. hubiera (hubiese) partido
 3. comías
 4. hayamos hablado
 5. ¿hablasteis?
 6. partía
 7. aprenderemos
 8. tomaras (tomases)
 9. no escribiría
 10. comprendieron
 11. estás contestando
 12. habrían partido
 13. estabais hablando
 14. he estudiado
 15. ¡no acabéis!
 16. habían partido
 17. habré enseñado
 18. Ud. habrá vivido
 19. estamos viviendo
 20. Uds. habrían enseñado
 21. temamos
 22. no lees
 23. vendiera (vendiese)
 24. no hayáis comido
 25. estaba vendiendo

26. no hubierais (hubieseis) escuchado
27. vendo
28. ¿leerás?
29. llevaban
30. escribiste
31. asistiréis
32. tomaríamos
33. no está estudiando
34. estabais abriendo
35. Ud. no ha asistido
36. había comprendido
37. llevarías
38. habrán estudiado
39. Uds. no habrían necesitado
40. !beban!
41. no asistiéramos (asistiésemos)
42. has vivido
43. haya acabado
44. Uds. hubieran (hubiesen) aprendido
45. ¿abrís?
46. temía
47. habías tomado
48. preguntaron
49. Ud. entrará
50. ¿leerías?

STEM-CHANGING VERBS—CLASS I

p. 63

(1) piense, peinses, piense, piense, pensemos, penséis, piensen, piensen,

(2) entienda, entiendas, entienda, entienda, entendamos, entendáis, entiendan, entiendan.

(1) cuento, cuentas, cuenta, cuenta, contamos, contáis, cuentan, cuentan,

(2) vuelvo, vuelves, vuelve, vuelve, volvemos, volvéis, vuelven, vuelven.

146

Para practicar

p. 64

A.

cierro, encuentro, muestro, pierdo, revuelvo, enciendo.

confiesan, se acuestan, mueven, devuelven, aciertan, acuerdan.

nos sentamos, contamos, mostramos, perdemos, devolvemos, entendemos.

B.

cuentes, pienses, muerdas, apruebes, devuelvas, entiendas.

cierren, encuentren, muestren, pierdan, muevan, enciendan.

entendáis, revolváis, mostréis, mováis, confeséis, acordéis.

Mastery Test

p. 65

A.
1. they go to bed
2. I remember
3. she returns
4. you may warm
5. we may show
6. you lose
7. you may stir (turnover)
8. you may burn
9. he approved
10. I used to sit
11. it cost
12. it will snow
13. I confess
14. they give back
15. close

B.
1. perdisteis
2. entiendan
3. encontremos
4. ¿cierras?
5. no entiendes
6. movieron
7. estaba moviendo
8. muestren
9. mueves
10. calentamos
11. estoy encendiendo
12. no pierden
13. muerda
14. revuelvas
15. cuesta-

STEM-CHANGING VERBS—CLASS II
Para practicar

pp. 67—68

adviertes, mientes, mueres, hieres, consientes

se divierta, sienta, duerma, mienta, muera

hirieron, advirtieron, se divirtieron, durmieron, consintieron

muriéramos (muriésemos), sintiéramos (sintiésemos), mintiéramos (mintiésemos), durmiéramos (durmiésemos), advirtiéramos (advirtiésemos)

muriendo, hiriendo, consintiendo, advirtiendo, divirtiéndose

Mastery Test

p. 68

A.
1. you used to lie
2. we sleep (slept)
3. she died
4. they might lie
5. he had felt
6. they have fun
7. he wounded
8. he may consent
9. I do not notice
10. you lied
11. I felt
12. you may die
13. you may feel
14. they may sleep
15. we may have fun

B.
1. no hieren
2. has dormido
3. consintamos
4. muriera (muriese)
5. duerma
6. te divertiste
7. mentiremos
8. estaban muriendo
9. estaba sintiendo
10. durmiera (durmiese)
11. consentiría
12. Ud. advirtió
13. duermo
14. sintieran (sintiesen)
15. os divirtáis

STEM-CHANGING VERBS-CLASS III

Para practicar

pp. 69-70

impide, compites, sirves, mides

gimáis, pidáis, impidáis, compitáis

se vistieron, sirvieron, midieron, impidieron.

Mastery Test

p. 70

1. they might groan
2. I may dress
3. he would ask for
4. we used to measure
5. you may measure
6. we prevent
7. you groaned
8. I will compete
9. we might serve
10. he groans
11. you measured
12. they served
13. I compete
14. they get dressed
15. you may prevent

Repaso (Stem-changing verbs)

pp. 70-71

A.

gime, compite, cierra, siente, impide, muestra, encuentra, se divierte, se sienta, revuelve.

B.

aprobemos, midamos, durmamos, confesemos, mintamos, advirtamos, pidamos, nos vistamos, repitamos, consintamos.

C.

1. entienden
2. consintamos
3. me vista
4. no se está divirtiendo (no está divirtiéndose)
5. cerremos
6. pediste
7. no advirtió
8. encuentra
9. Ud. gimiera
10. muera
11. muevas
12. sirviéramos (sirviésemos)
13. advierten
14. cierro
15. compite
16. muestres
17. me divirtiera (divirtiese)
18. sirvieron
19. no perdís
20. duerma
21. impide
22. devuelva
23. sintieron
24. Uds. impidan
25. ¿entiende?
26. no están muriendo (no mueren)
27. no compitió
28. nieve
29. estás mintiendo (mientes)
30. pidieran (pidiesen)

ORTHOGRAPHIC CHANGES

Para practicar

pp. 74–75

seques, coloques, obligues, entregues, amenaces, analices, averigües, mengües.

alcancen, abracen, lleguen, castiguen, arriesguen, rasquen, repliquen, expliquen.

expliqué, saqué, indiqué, negué, llegué, castigué, rogué, repliqué, empecé, crucé, rechacé, almorcé, margué, apacigüé, santigüé.

Mastery Test

pp. 75–76

A. 1. he may explain
    2. you might mark
    3. I may turn off
    4. I embraced
    5. I handed over
    6. we may stumble
    7. they may dry
    8. you may punish
    9. you may reject
    10. you may find out
    11. you may reply
    12. we may load
    13. you may threaten
    14. I decreased
    15. I took out
    16. we may bless
    17. he may arrive
    18. you may analyze
    19. they may pacify
    20. he may reach (achieve)

B. 1. apacigüemos
    2. pagué
    3. saquen
    4. no averigüé
    5. castigues
    6. no coloque
    7. arriesgué
    8. fatiguemos
    9. non replique
    10. cruces
    11. roguéis
    12. indiqué
    13. reza
    14. lances
    15. lleguen
    16. no expliqué
    17. no analicemos
    18. repliquéis
    19. lancé
    20. sollocé

Para practicar

p. 78

encojo, dirijo, cojo, exijo, ejerzo, convenzo, esparzo, extingo, delinco, acojo.

extingamos, delincamos, distingamos, escojamos, inflijamos, finjamos, cojamos, esparzamos, ejerzamos, dirijamos.

Aplicación

p. 79

1. I exercise
2. you convinced
3. I will scatter
4. you used to welcome
5. they may distinguish
6. we may pretend
7. you have convinced
8. I will direct
9. he would follow
10. you may extinguish
11. you used to exercise
12. I demand
13. I followed
14. you extinguished
15. they may convince
16. I pretended
17. he broke the law
18. they may catch (seize)
19. I extinguish
20. you may break the law

Mastery Test

pp. 79–80

1. vencieras (vencieses)
2. inflija
3. distingo
4. ejercimos
5. no exijo
6. no distingas
7. no convencerá
8. ¿escogerán Uds? (¿elegirán Uds.?)
9. no extingamos
10. esparcí
11. dirigimos
12. distinguió
13. delinco
14. ejerces
15. acoja
16. extingan
17. no convenzan
18. finjo
19. distinguiréis
20. no relincas

Para practicar

p. 82

aparezcas, ofrezcas, merezcas, reconozcas, compadezcas, confíes, guíes, descontinúes.

desafío, parezco, obedezco, agradezco, insinúo, desconfío.

leyeron, poseyeron, enviaron, continuaron, conocieron, ofrecieron.

Aplicación

p. 83

1. estamos leyendo
2. enviáis
3. continuéis
4. ofrecemos
5. Uds. desafíen
6. aborrezcáis
7. merezcamos
8. Uds. aparezcan
9. guiamos
10. desconocieron
11. poseyeron
12. Uds. insinúen
13. se enriquezcan
14. parecimos
15. nos habituamos
16. creyésemos
17. Uds. complacían
18. ellas desconfían
19. descontinuamos
20. reconocemos

Mastery Test

pp. 83–84

1. ¿leyó?
2. desaparezcamos
3. continúe
4. envíen
5. poseía
6. Ud. no conozca
7. desconfiemos
8. no guío
9. leyeras
10. compadezca
11. enviaba
12. descontinúes
13. creíamos
14. desaparecéis
15. enviaron
16. no creyó
17. aborrecí
18. ¿confías?
19. conozcan
20. continuó

ORTHOGRAPHIC STEM CHANGES

Para practicar

pp. 87–89

corrijo, ruego, ciego, tropiezo, consigo, construyo, sonrío.

desniega, persigue, ríe, destruye, se esfuerza, elige, juega.

colegí, rogué, almorcé, incluí, reí, proseguí, cegué.

corrigieron, consiguieron, sonrieron, restituyeron, eligieron, instruyeron, negaron.

ciegues, juegues, tropieces, corrijas, prosigas, destruyas, rías.

desneguemos, nos esforcemos, elijamos, consigamos, sonriamos, concluyamos, juguemos.

corrigiera (corrigiese), prosiguiera (prosiguiese), riera (riese), construyera (construyese), eligiera (eligiese), constituyera (constituyese), consiguiera (consiguiese).

coligiendo, colgando, almorzando, sonriendo, destruyendo, persiguiendo.

cegado, empezado, elegido, seguido, reído, concluido, huido.

Aplicación

pp. 89−90

1. rueguen Uds.
2. tropezamos
3. ellos almuercen
4. cegamos
5. escogemos
6. empezamos
7. jugamos
8. nos esforzamos
9. colgáis
10. empezamos
11. huyen
12. Uds. sonrieron
13. ellos destruyeron
14. concluyésemos
15. habéis huido
16. ellos corrijan
17. Uds. consiguieron
18. seguimos
19. escogiéramos
20. consigáis
21. estaban siguiendo
22. elijamos
23. corregimos
24. persiguen
25. incluyáis
26. concluíamos
27. Uds. habían reído
28. instruímos
29. Uds. han restituido
30. están sonriendo

Mastery Test

pp. 90−91

A.
1. I may turn off
2. I exercise
3. you send
4. I stumble
5. extinguish!
6. I offer
7. I handed over
8. they may distinguish
9. you may be unacquainted
10. I played
11. we may pretend
12. I guide
13. you may eat lunch
14. I correct
15. he possessed
16. you may reply
17. they may catch
18. you may insinuate
19. you may threaten
20. I demand
21. I might believe
22. I marked
23. you may get
24. I smile
25. you may beg
26. they may convince
27. you might conclude
28. you may pacify
29. you may break the law
30. he destroyed

B.
1. pagué
2. escogiera (escogiese); eligiera (eligiese)
3. ¿leyo?
4. no averigüé
5. siguieron
6. continúe
7. no coloque
8. no extingas
9. envíen
10. lleguemos
11. ¿consiguió Ud.?
12. no conozcas
13. Ud. cruce
14. sigo
15. no guío
16. rogué
17. delinco
18. leyeras (leyeses)
19. empecéis
20. dirija
21. destruyeron
22. no expliqué
23. finjo
24. no te ríes
25. Ud. replique
26. no convenzan
27. creíamos
28. lancé
29. escojas (elijas)
30. concluyéramos (concluyésemos)

Repaso general 1

pp. 92–93

A. 1. partimos
2. comprendisteis
3. vivían
4. asistiremos
5. tomaríais
6. estamos escribiendo
7. estabn vistiéndose
8. hemos hablado
9. Uds. habían vendido
10. habréis asistido
11. habrían bebido
12. contesten Uds.
13. aprendierais
14. hayan entrado
15. hubiéramos tomado
16. acordamos
17. se acuesten
18. consintamos
19. no se divierten
20. Uds. pidieron
21. leyeron
22. rieron
23. negamos
24. Uds. incluyan
25. juguéis
26. reconocemos
27. Uds. persiguieron
28. almorcéis
29. averiguamos
30. distinguimos

B. 1. temen
2. bebías
3. mostréis
4. empecé
5. ¿hablaste?
6. sirvieron
7. creíamos
8. leyerais
9. no escribiría
10. advierte
11. convenzan
12. no empiece
13. hablabas
14. nieva
15. Uds. expliquen
16. dirijáis
17. habré enseñado
18. pidieran
19. no te ríes
20. no guío
21. temamos
22. escojo
23. ¿continúas?
24. no expliqué
25. vendía
26. rogué
27. destruyeron
28. escojas
29. llevaban
30. envía

Repaso general 2

pp. 93–95

A. 1. había temido
2. he partido
3. habían vivido
4. habré necesitado
5. habríamos partido
6. hayas comido
7. habiésemos vendido
8. Ud. había reído
9. has restituido
10. han enviado
11. he descontinuado
12. he obedecido

B. 1. habrían partido
2. lean
3. concluyéramos (concluyésemos)
4. no está estudiando
5. comprenden
6. pagué
7. cruces
8. Ud. llevaría
9. cerremos
10. escogiera (escogiese); eligiera (eligiese)
11. ¿conseguiste?
12. no asistiéramos (asistiésemos)

13. había creído
14. hayan desaparecido
15. yo hubiera poseído
16. ha tropezado
17. haya distinguido
18. han jugado
19. hayan explicado
20. he conseguido
21. había herido
22. has elegido
23. él haya delinquido
24. han sonreído
25. habían destruido
26. habréis hablado
27. había aprendido
28. había dormido
29. hubiéramos corregido
30. hubiera huido

13. impidierais (impidieseis)
14. ¿leyó?
15. lleguemos
16. ¿abre Ud.?
17. impidieron
18. no averigüé
19. no cruzáis
20. entrarás
21. me visto
22. siguieron
23. cierro
24. ¿leerían Uds.?
25. mueran
26. !continúen!
27. sigo
28. Uds. habrán vivido
29. perdáis
30. no busque

IRREGULAR VERBS

Para practicar

pp. 97−98

desasgo, quepo, ando, decaigo

asen, andan, caen, caben

desasió, cupo, anduvo, cayó

asiremos, decaeremos, cabremos, andaremos

desasgas, caigas, quepas, andes

descayerais (decayeseis), anduvierais (anduvieseis), cupierais (cupieseis), asierais (asieseis)

Aplicación

p. 98

1. they would fall
2. we will fit
3. you may have fallen
4. you were walking
5. you would fit
6. they fell
7. you would decline
8. you fit
9. we loosen
10. we walked
11. we may decline
12. they may fit
13. you may fall
14. I will seize
15. we were declining
16. he will fall
17. I might fit
18. I fall
19. I fit
20. they may seize
21. you might decline
22. we will walk
23. they might have seized
24. they would have walked
25. you will seize
26. they are declining
27. we may walk
28. he will have declined
29. they might walk
30. you seize

Mastery Test

pp. 99–100

1. no caerían
2. hubiera (hubiese) andado
3. asirían
4. ¿andabas?
5. decaen
6. desasieran (desasiesen)
7. decaeríais
8. ¿andaré?
9. desasgo
10. anduvo
11. ¿cupo?
12. desasíamos
13. decayeron
14. habríamos cabido
15. no caeré
16. cabe
17. anduviéramos (anduviésemos)
18. había asido
19. no habría caído
20. ande
21. habías asido
22. ando
23. Uds. caerían
24. ¿asió?
25. ha caído
26. quepamos
27. andabas
28. caíamos
29. hayas andado
30. habíamos cabido
31. haya asido
32. os caísteis
33. hubiera (hubiese) caído
34. Ud. cupo
35. cupiera (cupiese)
36. decaes
37. asgan
38. cayéramos (cayésemos)
39. no quepa
40. caigáis

Para practicar

p. 101

deduzco, maldigo, yerro, doy, traduzco.

produjeron, bendijeron, dieron, condujeron, erraron.

traducirá, maldecirá, deducirá, bendecirá, dará.

habían dado, habían deducido, habían bendecido, habían errado, habían dicho.

des, produzcas, bendigas, yerres, digas.

erráramos (errásemos), tradujéramos (tradujésemos), maldijéramos (maldijésemos), diéramos (diésemos), condujéramos (condujésemos).

Aplicación

pp. 102–03

1. you deduced
2. you give
3. he will say
4. we may wander
5. we used to lead
6. they may give
7. we may say
8. you were cursing
9. he translates
10. you would have given
11. they said
12. I may have said

13. she led
14. I give
15. you may wander
16. we would say
17. I may deduce
18. you gave
19. they bless
20. you wander
21. he would produce
22. you might give
23. he might say
24. I wander
25. she might translate
26. we were giving
27. they would have cursed
28. I wandered
29. I produce
30. I will give

Mastery Test

pp. 103–04

1. dirás
2. conducís
3. erremos
4. haya dicho
5. no daba
6. tradujiste
7. bendiga
8. daremos
9. Uds. produzcan
10. ¿condujo?
11. no dijerais
12. ¿da?
13. yerro
14. dedujera (dedujese)
15. maldeciríamos
16. dieron
17. produjera (produjese)
18. ¡no traduzcan!
19. ¿están diciendo?
20. erraron
21. hubieran (hubiesen) dado
22. ¿no habéis dicho?
23. produzco
24. yerra
25. no diremos
26. no decían
27. no doy
28. deduzca
29. no traduzcan
30. maldijiste
31. ¿disteis?
32. conduciremos
33. Ud. dé
34. bendigo
35. produjeron
36. traducías
37. no diera
38. maldiga
39. hayan dado
40. no conduzca

Para practicar

pp. 105–06

1. vamos
2. Uds. satisfagan
3. habrán
4. estamos
5. ibais
6. nosotros hubiéramos
7. hemos
8. estuvieron
9. fuimos
10. harán
11. hubisteis
12. hicierais
13. ellos vayan
14. estuvierais
15. habéis hecho
16. Uds. hayan
17. fuerais
18. satisficieron
19. Uds. estén
20. satisfacemos

Aplicación

p. 106

1. he will have satisfied
2. we are
3. there is (are)
4. you went
5. he would do
6. you satisfied
7. there would have been
8. you may have done
9. I would not be
10. I will satisfy
11. they had
12. we used to do (make)
13. you were going
14. we might satisfy
15. there may have been

16. I would have been
17. you may satisfy
18. you might be
19. you would have
20. we did
21. they were
22. he might do
23. he has
24. you may not go
25. I would have done
26. you were satisfying
27. we might go
28. they may be
29. I was
30. he goes

Mastery Test

pp. 107–08

1. hubiéramos (hubiésemos) ido
2. estuve
3. haya hecho
4. habrían satisfecho
5. estaba
6. no habrán ido
7. no hacíamos
8. Uds. satisfarán
9. estamos
10. había hecho
11. iba
12. satisfice
13. estemos
14. no hay
15. no satisfacemos
16. ¿va?
17. Ud. estará
18. hicieron
19. satisfagamos
20. no estuviera (estuviese)

21. habría habido
22. fueras
23. satisfacía
24. habrá
25. vaya
26. hubiera (hubiese) habido
27. satisfaga
28. harás
29. hubiera (hubiese)
30. hubieran (hubiesen) estado
31. fuisteis
32. ha habido
33. no hagan
34. satisfago
35. hubieran (hubiesen) hecho
36. no iré
37. haya
38. haríamos
39. había
40. no estoy

Para practicar

pp. 109–10

propones, hueles, puedes, oyes, compones.

dispusieron, pudieron, oyeron, impusieron, supusieron.

dispondré, expondré, impondré, propondré, supondré.

componga, pueda, oiga, huela, exponga.

hayamos oído, hayamos dispuesto, hayamos puesto, hayamos supuesto, hayamos podido.

Aplicación

p. 110

1. pusieran
2. podamos
3. oirían
4. pudisteis
5. disponéis
6. oíamos
7. Uds. podrán
8. olieron
9. hemos compuesto
10. habremos podido
11. oiremos
12. oleríais
13. impondrían
14. podían
15. habrán oído

16. huelen
17. expongamos
18. oyeron
19. pudiéramos
20. hayamos propuesto
21. podríais
22. oigáis
23. olemos
24. supondréis
25. podéis
26. Uds. oyen
27. oláis
28. dispusieron
29. oliéramos
30. hubierais puesto

Mastery Test

p. 111

1. oíste
2. no habíamos podido
3. huela
4. no habría puesto
5. no estabais oyendo (no oíais)
6. están imponiendo
7. pude
8. ¿huele?
9. oirían
10. pueda
11. habré compuesto
12. ¿pone?
13. ¿oye?
14. no expondrás
15. propongan

16. no pudiera (pudiese)
17. hubiéramos (hubiésemos) oído
18. Uds. podrían
19. olieran (oliesen)
20. supongamos
21. no oiréis
22. ¿puedes?
23. dispusiéramos (dispusiésemos)
24. no pondrán
25. oyeron
26. pudisteis
27. suponía
28. podrás
29. no oyéramos (oyésemos)
30. ¿expusisteis?

Aplicación

pp. 113-14

A.
1. fuimos (éramos)
2. supeiras (supieses)
3. salimos (salíamos)
4. supo (sabía)
5. fuiste (eras)
6. saliera (saliese)
7. fuera (fuese)
8. fui (era)
9. quisimos (queríamos)
10. salí (salía)
11. había sabido
12. habíais salido
13. quiso (quería)
14. estabas saliendo
15. quisieran (quisiesen)

B.
1. salíamos
2. Uds. sabrán
3. querréis
4. salieron
5. sepáis
6. saldríais
7. saben
8. sois
9. habíamos querido
10. salgan
11. serán
12. quisieran
13. saldremos
14. seamos
15. Uds. fueran

C.
1. we would be
2. we were
3. you wanted
4. I will have been
5. you might be
6. I have known
7. we will have known
8. we may want
9. you will know
10. you were
11. he knew
12. he had gone out
13. they were wanting
14. they would know
15. they may have left
16. we might have known
17. I may be
18. he might want
19. they might leave
20. we might know

Mastery Test

pp. 114-15

1. supiera
2. habéis salido
3. querría
4. no fui
5. habéis sabido
6. somos
7. salga
8. querrás
9. sabíamos
10. era
11. queríamos
12. no saliéramos (saliésemos)
13. sabréis
14. sean
15. haya querido
16. Ud. no será
17. habrán sabido
18. salieron
19. habías querido
20. no salimos
21. haya sabido
22. ¿es?
23. salías
24. no quise
25. habrían sabido
26. ¿no quieren?
27. hemos sido
28. saldrá
29. sabríamos
30. Uds. quisieran (quisiesen)

31. salgo
32. Ud. supo
33. he querido
34. hubiéramos (hubiésemos) sido
35. quieras

36. ¿saldrían?
37. sé
38. fuera
39. fueron
40. habremos sido

Para practicar

p. 117

contraigo, convengo, detengo, mantengo, sostengo.

mantiene, viene, vale, retiene, trae.

convendrán, detendrán, mantendrán, valdrán,
sostendrán.

contuvo, trajo, convino, sostuvo, detuvo.

vengas, mantengas, contraigas, contengas, valgas.

contrajéramos (contrajésemos), viniéramos
(viniésemos), tuviéramos (tuviésemos), sostuviéramos (sostuviésemos), mantuviéramos (mantuviésemos).

Aplicación

p. 118

1. he will have come
2. you may have brought
3. they had
4. we may be worth
5. they will bring
6. I had
7. we would be worth
8. they had come
9. we used to have
10. you would bring
11. you have been worth
12. you come
13. you will be worth
14. he might come
15. I brought

16. I will have
17. he might be worth
18. they might have
19. he has brought
20. they may come
21. they used to bring
22. you would have
23. we were worth
24. we will have come
25. you may bring
26. you have
27. I would be worth
28. you might have
29. we might bring
30. you were coming

Mastery Test

pp. 118–19

1. no ha vendio
2. había tenido
3. trajeras
4. valió
5. hubiéramos (hubiésemos) tenido
6. habían traido
7. vinisteis
8. traía
9. tuvo
10. valen
11. no tendrían
12. trajo
13. venían
14. ¿tienes?
15. traigan
16. venga
17. no estamos trayendo
18. tendremos
19. valdrás
20. ¿tenéis?
21. no traigas
22. vengo
23. Uds. tengan
24. no valgo
25. hayas venido
26. no traería
27. tuvieron
28. trajeron
29. ¿vendrán?
30. tuvierais
31. valiera (valiese)
32. tenías
33. traigamos
34. ha tenido
35. has traído
36. ¿no tuvieron?
37. no valdría
38. estáis trayendo
39. viniéramos (viniésemos)
40. trajera

IRREGULAR PAST PARTICIPLES

Aplicación

p. 120

1. I may see
2. they might have discovered
3. we might see
4. you may have seen
5. you would see
6. we saw
7. we have described
8. he may see
9. he will have died
10. you were seeing
11. you will see
12. I had resolved
13. we see
14. you saw
15. they would have returned

Mastery Test

pp. 120–21

1. no vemos
2. veían
3. vierais (vieseis)
4. no había escrito
5. veas
6. no vio
7. ¿han descubierto?
8. hubiera visto
9. veríamos
10. no ha cubierto
11. veía
12. no verá
13. haya visto
14. habrían abierto
15. ¿no veis?

Repaso de verbos irregulares

pp. 121–23

A. 1. he will have come
2. you had
3. they would go
4. you will say
5. you went (were)
6. he would want
7. we see
8. I was (went)
9. I brought
10. he was going out
11. you will have known
12. they might be
13. we had been able
14. I would have put
15. they may give
16. I may walk
17. they might fall
18. we may be worth
19. he had fit
20. you heard
21. he will have satisfied
22. he would not do
23. we lead
24. you would seize
25. you used to translate

26. there may have been
27. she says
28. we go
29. we had been
30. you will have
31. they used to come
32. they may have seen
33. you wanted
34. he used to bring
35. they gave
36. you may be
37. you used to go out
38. you used to put
39. we can
40. we will know
41. we had heard
42. you will be worth
43. I may have done
44. you will satisfy
45. I will fall
46. she walked
47. he may fit
48. there will be
49. they translated
50. I may lead

B. 1. sean
2. habremos venido
3. decías
4. ¿va?
5. viéramos (viésemos)
6. tuvieran
7. habías querido
8. traería
9. sepa
10. estamos
11. habrás puesto
12. podía
13. no hemos dado
14. no salió
15. hayáis caído
16. oíamos
17. cayó
18. valdríamos
19. anduvo
20. cupe
21. no haré
22. traducían
23. habrían asido
24. condujo
25. deduzcas

26. habría
27. habrá dicho
28. iría
29. hayan visto
30. tengan
31. venía
32. quería
33. habéis sido
34. no traigamos
35. no sabe
36. pudiste
37. estaremos
38. ¡den!
39. saldría
40. pondréis
41. oiga
42. no andaremos
43. cabré
44. Ud. ha valido
45. satisficiéramos (satisficiésemos)
46. no hicimos
47. caigo
48. asgamos
49. hubieran (hubiesen) sido
50. condujera (condujese)

Repaso general 2

pp. 123–25

A. 1. we think
    2. you opened
    3. they may lose
    4. she answers
    5. I understand
    6. I arrived
    7. you will say
    8. he had fun
    9. I sleep
  10. we brought
  11. I did
  12. they will come
  13. you may know
  14. I might put
  15. we may be able

  16. you may choose
  17. we might return
  18. they may take out
  19. they distinguish
  20. I might look for
  21. I will read
  22. you would know
  23. they will have
  24. I gave
  25. you will see
  26. he insinuates
  27. I may begin
  28. we send (sent)
  29. I may have played
  30. I may trust

B. 1. escribíamos
    2. entiende
    3. viven
    4. viajaban (estaban viajando)
    5. guardas
    6. traían (estaban trayendo)
    7. ¿decimos?
    8. quiere
    9. se vistió
  10. no vieron
  11. salimos
  12. pusiera (pusiese)
  13. no han hecho
  14. no sé
  15. pudiste

  16. dirigimos
  17. busqué
  18. escogieran (escogiesen), eligieran (eligiesen)
  19. ¡expliquen!
  20. llegue
  21. vales
  22. ¿leyeron?
  23. dieras (dieses)
  24. no vayamos
  25. tenga
  26. jueguen
  27. negué
  28. continúe
  29. no empecé
  30. envíen

Repaso general 3

pp. 125–26

A. 1. I began
    2. I may play
    3. we were denying
    4. she continues
    5. they will send

    6. you get
    7. I had
    8. you led
    9. I was going out
  10. they knew (found out)

11. he would smell
12. you fit
13. he may put
14. we would be able
15. I come
16. they will have died
17. I was laughing
18. he was contributing
19. he destroys
20. you used to possess

21. they may construct
22. he loses
23. we were serving
24. he used to know
25. she wounded
26. I may think
27. they threw
28. he will have lost
29. you were listening
30. she had returned

B. 1. jugabais
2. empezaran (empezasen)
3. continúo
4. confié
5. no leen
6. no quiso
7. serían
8. no corrijo
9. fui
10. dijo
11. vea
12. Ud. caía
13. hice
14. he puesto
15. saldrán

16. lea
17. habíamos dormido
18. riéramos (riésemos)
19. muera
20. no creyeron
21. envié
22. ¿consentís?
23. destruyan
24. repetía
25. perdíamos
26. no vuelves (devuelves)
27. pasábamos
28. vivía
29. entendisteis
30. han abierto

Index of Infinitives

A

achieve alcanzar, 73
admire admirar, 24
adorn adornar, 24
agree acordar, 73; convenir, 117
amuse (oneself) divertirse, 67
analyze analizar, 73
answer contestar, 6
appear aparecer, 81
approve aprobar, 63
arise, get up levantarse, 54–56
arrive llegar, 73
ask preguntar, 6
ask for pedir, 69; rogar, 73, 85
attend asistir, 6

B

be ser, 113; estar, 104
be able poder, 108–09
be acquainted conocer, 81
be suitable convenir, 117
be unacquainted desconocer, 81
be worth valer, 116
become rich enriquecerse, 81
beg rogar, 73, 85
begin empezar, 73, 85
believe creer, 6, 80
bite morder, 63
bless bendecir, 101; santiguar, 74
blind cegar, 73, 85
bother molestar, 24
break the law delinquir, 78
bring traer, 116
burn encender, 63
buy comprar, 9

C

call llamar, 24
call together convocar, 72
can, be able poder, 108–09
carry llevar, 4
catch coger, 77
challenge desafiar, 81
chew mascar, masticar, 72
choose escoger, 77; elegir, 77, 86
clean limpiar, 24
close cerrar, 63

collect colegir, 86
comb (oneself) peinarse, 56
come venir, 116–17
compete competir, 69
compose componer, 109
conclude concluir, 87
conduct conducir, 100
confess confesar, 63
conquer vencer, 76
consent consentir, 67
constitute constituir, 87
construct construir, 87
contain contener, 116
continue continuar, 82; seguir, 86
contract contraer, 116
contradict desnegar, 85
convince convencer, 76
correct corregir, 77, 86
cost costar, 63
cover cubrir, 24, 120
cross cruzar, 73
curse maldecir, 101

D

decide decidir, 24
decline decaer, 97
decrease menguar, 74
deduce deducir, 100
defy desafiar, 81
demand exigir, 77
deny negar, 73, 85
describe describir, 120
deserve merecer, 81
destroy destruir, 87
die morir, 67, 120
direct dirigir, 77
disappear desaparecer, 81
discontinue descontinuar, 82
discover descubrir, 120
discuss discutir, 24
dispose disponer, 109
distinguish distinguir, 77
do hacer, 105
dress (oneself) vestirse, 69
drink beber, 2, 6
drown ahogar, 73
dry secar, 72

O

obey   obedecer, 81
oblige   obligar, 73
obtain   conseguir, 77, 86
offend   ofender, 24
offer   ofrecer, 81
open   abrir, 6, 120

P

pacify   apaciguar, 74
pass   pasar, 18
pay   pagar, 72–73
persecute   perseguir, 77, 86
pity   compadecer, 81
place, put   colocar, 72; poner, 109
play   jugar, 85
please   complacer, 81
pray   rogar, 73, 85; rezar, 73
prepare   preparar, 18
pretend   fingir, 77
prevent   impedir, 69
produce   producir, 100
propose   proponer, 109
prosecute   proseguir, 77, 86
punish   castigar, 73
pursue   perseguir, 77, 86
put, place   poner, 109; colocar, 72

R

rain   llover, 63
read   leer, 6, 80
reach   alcanzar, 73
receive   recibir, 3, 6
recognize   reconocer, 81
reject   rechazer, 73
remember   acordar(se), 63
repeat   repetir, 69
reply   responder, 18; replicar, 72; contestar, 6
return   volver, 62, 120; devolver, 63, 120
revolve   revolver, 63, 120
risk   arriesgar, 73
run   correr, 18

S

satisfy   satisfacer, 105
say, tell   decir, 101
scatter   esparcir, 76
scratch   rascar, 72
see   ver, 119

seem   parecer, 81
seize   asir, 96; coger, 77
sell   vender, 2, 6
send   enviar, 81
serve   servir, 69
show   enseñar, 6; mostrar, 63
shrink   encoger, 77
sin   pecar, 72
sit   sentarse, 63
sleep   dormir, 66–67
smell   oler, 108
smile   sonreír, 87
snow   nevar, 63
sob   sollozar, 73
speak   hablar, 1, 8, 13, 20, 26, 31, 36–37, 42, 46, 49
spend   pasar, 18
stir   revolver, 63, 120
stop   detener, 116
study   estudiar, 6
stumble   tropezar, 73, 86
succeed   acertar, 63; conseguir, 77, 86
suppose   suponer, 109
sustain   sostener, 116

T

take   tomar, 2, 6; coger, 77
take out   sacar, 72
teach   enseñar, 6
tell   contar, 62; decir, 101
thank   agradecer, 81
think   pensar, 62
threaten   amenazer, 73
throw   echar, 18; lanzar, 73
tire   fatigar, 73
translate   traducir, 100
travel   viajar, 18
trust   confiar, 81
try hard   esforzarse, 86
turn off   apagar, 73
turnover   revolver, 63, 120

U

understand   comprender, 16; entender, 62
undertake   emprender, 24
unite   unir, 6

W

walk   andar, 96
wander   errar, 101; vagar, 73

FOREIGN LANGUAGE BOOKS AND MATERIALS

Spanish
Vox Spanish and English Dictionaries
Cervantes-Walls Spanish and English Dictionary
NTC's Dictionary of Spanish False Cognates
Complete Handbook of Spanish Verbs
Guide to Spanish Suffixes
Nice 'n Easy Spanish Grammar
Spanish Verbs and Essentials of Grammar
Spanish Verb Drills
Getting Started in Spanish
Guide to Spanish Idioms
Guide to Correspondence in Spanish
Diccionario Básico Norteamericano
Diccionario del Español Chicano
Basic Spanish Conversation
Let's Learn Spanish Picture Dictionary
My First Spanish and English Dictionary
Spanish Picture Dictionary
Welcome to Spain
Spanish for Beginners
Spanish à la Cartoon
El alfabeto
Let's Sing and Learn in Spanish
Let's Learn Spanish Coloring Book
Let's Learn Spanish Coloring Book-Audiocassette Package
My World in Spanish Coloring Book
Easy Spanish Word Games and Puzzles
Easy Spanish Crossword Puzzles
Easy Spanish Vocabulary Puzzles
Easy Spanish Word Power Games
How to Pronounce Spanish Correctly

French
NTC's New College French and English Dictionary
NTC's Dictionary of *Faux Amis*
NTC's Dictionary of Canadian French
French Verbs and Essentials of Grammar
Real French
Getting Started in French
Guide to French Idioms
Guide to Correspondence in French
Nice 'n Easy French Grammar
French à la Cartoon
French for Beginners
Let's Learn French Picture Dictionary
French Picture Dictionary
Welcome to France
The French-Speaking World
L'alphabet
Let's Learn French Coloring Book
Let's Learn French Coloring Book-Audiocassette Package
My World in French Coloring Book
French Verb Drills
Easy French Crossword Puzzles
Easy French Vocabulary Games
Easy French Grammar Puzzles
Easy French Word Games
Easy French Culture Games
How to Pronounce French Correctly
L'Express: Ainsi va la France
L'Express: Aujourd'hui la France
Le Nouvel Observateur: Arts, idées, spectacles
Au courant: Expressions for Communicating in
  Everyday French

Audio and Video Language Programs
Just Listen 'n Learn: Spanish, French, Italian,
  German, Greek, and Arabic
Just Listen 'n Learn PLUS: Spanish, French,
  and German
Conversational...in 7 Days: Spanish, French,
  German, Italian, Rusian, Greek, Portuguese
Practice & Improve Your...Spanish, French,
  German, and Italian
Practice & Improve Your...Spanish, French,
  German, and Italian PLUS
Improve Your...Spanish, French,
  German, and Italian: The P&I Method
VideoPassport French and Spanish

German
Schöffler-Weis German and English Dictionary
Klett German and English Dictionary
Das Max und Moritz Buch
NTC's Dictionary of German False Cognates
Getting Started in German
German Verbs and Essentials of Grammar
Guide to German Idioms
Street-wise German
Nice 'n Easy German Grammar
German à la Cartoon
Let's Learn German Picture Dictionary
German Picture Dictionary
German for Beginners
German Verb Drills
Easy German Crossword Puzzles
Easy German Word Games and Puzzles
Let's Learn German Coloring Book
Let's Learn German Coloring Book-Audiocassette Package
My World in German Coloring Book
How to Pronounce German Correctly
Der Spiegel: Aktuelle Themen in der
  Bundesrepublik Deutschland

Italian
Zanichelli Super-Mini Italian and Dictionary
Zanichelli New College Italian and English Dictionary
Basic Italian Conversation
Getting Started in Italian
Italian Verbs and Essentials of Grammar
Let's Learn Italian Picture Dictionary
My World in Italian Coloring Book
Let's Learn Italian Coloring Book
Let's Learn Italian Coloring Book-Audiocassette Package
How to Pronounce Italian Correctly

Greek and Latin
NTC's New College Greek and English Dictionary
Essentials of Latin Grammar

Russian
Complete Handbook of Russian Verbs
Basic Structure Practice in Russian
Essentials of Russian Grammar
Business Russian
Roots of the Russian Language
Inspector General
Reading and Translating Contemporary Russian
How to Pronounce Russian

Polish
The Wiedza Powszechna Compact Polish and English
  Dictionary

Hebrew
Everyday Hebrew

Japanese
101 Japanese Idioms
Japanese in Plain English
Everyday Japanese
Japanese for Children
Japan Today!
Easy Hiragana
Easy Katakana
Easy Kana Workbook
How to Pronounce Japanese Correctly

Korean
Korean in Plain English

Chinese
Easy Chinese Phrasebook and Dictionary
Basic Chinese Vocabulary

Swedish
Swedish Verbs and Essentials of Grammar

Ticket to...Series
France, Germany, Spain, Italy (Guidebook and
  Audiocassette)

"Just Enough" Phrase Books
Chinese, Dutch, French, German, Greek, Hebrew,
  Hungarian, Italian, Japanese, Portuguese, Russian,
  Scandinavian, Serbo-Croat, Spanish
Business French, Business German, Business Spanish

PASSPORT BOOKS
a division of *NTC Publishing Group*
Lincolnwood, Illinois USA